FREDERICK WILLIAM MAITLAND

A BIOGRAPHICAL SKETCH

T0382404

Photogravure by Annan & Sons, Glasgow

Yours very truly,
F. W. Maitland

FREDERICK WILLIAM MAITLAND

DOWNING PROFESSOR OF THE LAWS OF ENGLAND

A BIOGRAPHICAL SKETCH

BY

H. A. L. FISHER

Cambridge :
at the University Press
1910

CAMBRIDGE UNIVERSITY PRESS
Cambridge, New York, Melbourne, Madrid, Cape Town,
Singapore, São Paulo, Delhi, Mexico City

Cambridge University Press
The Edinburgh Building, Cambridge CB2 8RU, UK

Published in the United States of America by Cambridge University Press, New York

www.cambridge.org
Information on this title: www.cambridge.org/9781107682146

First published 1910
First paperback edition 2013

A catalogue record for this publication is available from the British Library

ISBN 978-1-107-68214-6 Paperback

PREFATORY NOTE

WHATEVER merit this Memoir may possess it owes to Maitland and to the circle of those who cherish his memory. My own disabilities will be made plain to the reader, but, lest he entertain false expectations, let me explain at the outset that I was educated neither at Eton, nor at Cambridge, nor at Lincoln's Inn, that I am no lawyer, and that I have never received a formal education in the law. Finally, I did not make Maitland's acquaintance till he was in his thirty-seventh year. These are grave shortcomings, and if I do not rehearse the long roll of benefactors who have helped me to repair them, let it not be imputed to a failure in gratitude. I cannot, however, forbear from mentioning five names. Before these sheets went to Press they were read by Mrs Maitland, by Mrs Reynell, by Dr Henry Jackson, by Dr A. W. Verrall and by Professor Vinogradoff. To their intimate knowledge and weighty counsels I owe a deliverance from many errors. Dr Jackson has generously laid upon himself the additional burden of helping me to see the volume through the Press.

H. A. L. FISHER.

May 1910.

FREDERIC WILLIAM MAITLAND

I.

THE life of a great scholar may be filled with activity as intense and continuous as that demanded by any other calling, and yet is in the nature of things uneventful. Or rather it is a story which tells itself not in outward details of perils endured, places visited, appointments held, but in the revelation of the scholar's mind given in his work. Of such revelation there is no stint in the case of Frederic William Maitland. Within his brief span of life he crowded a mass of intellectual achievements which, if regard be had to its quality as well as to its volume, has hardly, if ever, been equalled in the history of English learning. And yet though a long array of volumes stands upon the Library shelves to give witness to Maitland's work, and not only to the work, but to the modest, brilliant and human spirit which shines through it all and makes it so different from the achievement of many learned men, some few words may be fitly said here as to his life and as to the place which he held and holds in our learning.

He was born on the 28th of May, 1850, at 53 Guilford Street, London, the only son of John Gorham Maitland and Emma Daniell. Father and mother both came of good intellectual lineage. John Gorham Maitland was the son of Samuel Roffey Maitland, the vigorous, learned and unconventional historian whose volume on the Dark Ages, published in 1844, dissipated a good deal of uncritical Protestant tradition. Emma Daniell was the daughter of John Frederic Daniell, a distinguished physicist, who became a Fellow of the Royal Society at the age of twenty-three, invented the hygrometer and published, as Professor of Chemistry at King's College, a well-known *Introduction to Chemical Philosophy*.

Such ancestry, at once historical and scientific, may explain some of Maitland's tastes and aptitudes. Indeed the words in which Dr Jessop has summarised the work of Samuel Maitland might be applied with equal propriety to the grandson. "Animated by a rare desire after simple truth, generously candid and free from all pretence or pedantry, he wrote in a style which was peculiarly sparkling, lucid and attractive." The secret of this stimulating and suggestive quality lay in the fact that Samuel Maitland was a man of independent mind who took nothing for granted and investigated things for himself. In 1891 his grandson wrote the following words to his eldest sister, who asked whether their grandfather's works would live. "Judging him merely as I should judge any other literary man I think him great. It seems to me that he did what was wanted just at the moment when it was wanted and so has a distinct place in the history of history in England. The *Facts and Documents* (illustrative of the History, Documents and Rites of the Ancient Albigenses and Waldenses) is the book that I admire most. Of course it is a book for the few, but then those few will be just the next generation of historians. It is a book which 'renders impossible' a whole class of existing books. I don't mean physically impossible—men will go on writing books of that class —but henceforth they will not be mistaken for great historians. One has still to do for legal history something of the work which S. R. M. did for ecclesiastical history—to teach men e.g. that some statement about the thirteenth century does not become the truer because it has been constantly repeated, that 'a chain of testimony' is never stronger than its first link. It is the 'method' that I admire in S. R. M. more even than the style or the matter—the application to remote events of those canons of evidence which we should all use about affairs of the present day, e.g. of the rule which excludes hearsay."

Cambridge and the bar were familiar traditions. Samuel Maitland was a member of Trinity College, Cambridge, who, having been called to the bar, abandoned the professional pursuit of the law for historical research. He took orders, became Librarian at Lambeth, and ultimately retired to Gloucester to read and to write. John Gorham, seventh wrangler, third classic, Chancellor's medallist, crowned a brilliant undergraduate career by a Fellowship in his father's college and was then called to the bar, but finding little practice drifted away into the Civil Service, becoming first, examiner, and afterwards, in succession to his friend

James Spedding, secretary to the Civil Service Commission, which last office he held till his death in 1863,
at the age of forty-five. That he could write with
point and vigour is made clear by a pamphlet upon the
Property and Income Tax, published in 1853, but the
work of the Civil Service Commission must have left
little leisure for writing, and early death cut short the
career of a man whose high gifts were as remarkable
to his friends as was the modesty with which he veiled
them from the world[1]. Frederic William, too, passed
from Cambridge to the law and then away to work
more congenial to his rare and original powers.

Of direct parental influence Maitland can have
known little. His mother died in 1851 when he
was a baby, and twelve years afterwards, six months
before a Brighton preparatory school was exchanged
for Eton, he and his two sisters were left fatherless
and the sole charge of the family devolved upon
Miss Daniell the aunt, who stood in a mother's place.
Dr Maitland, the historian, lived on till 1866 and his
home in Gloucester, still called Maitland House, was
from time to time enlivened by the visits of grand-
children. The fair landscape of Gloucestershire—the
wooded slopes of the Cotswolds, the rich pastures of
the Severn Valley with the silver thread of river
widening into a broad band as it nears the Bristol
Channel, the magical outline of the Malvern Hills, the
blaze of the nocturnal forges in the Forest of Dean,
were familiar to Maitland's boyhood. Gloucestershire
was his county, well-known and well-loved. The

---

[1] "The Cambridge Apostles," by W. D. Christie. *Macmillan's Magazine*, Nov. 1864.

beautiful old manor-house of Brookthorpe, one of those small grey-stone manor-houses which are the special pride of Gloucestershire, stood upon the lands which had come into the possession of the family through the marriage of Alexander Maitland with Caroline Busby in 1785. Round it in the parishes of Brookthorpe and Harescombe lay "Squire Maitland's" lands—a thriving cheese-making district until Canada began to filch away the favour of its Welsh customers.

Maitland was at Eton from 1863 to 1869, but failed to become prominent either in work or play. "He played football, was for a while a volunteer, rowed so much that he 'spoilt his style,' spent Sunday afternoons in running to St George's chapel to hear the anthem, and more than once began the holidays by walking home to Kensington[1]." Long afterwards when the question of compulsory Greek was being hotly debated in the Senate House at Cambridge he spoke with deep feeling of a "boy at school not more than forty years ago who was taught Greek for eight years and never learnt it...who reserved the greater part of his gratitude for a certain German governess...who if he never learnt Greek, did learn one thing, namely, to hate Greek and its alphabet and its accents and its accidence and its syntax and its prosody, and all its appurtenances; to long for the day when he would be allowed to learn something else; to vow that if ever he got rid of that accursed thing never, never again would he open a Greek book or write a Greek word[2]." We imagine a shy, awkward delicate boy bursting into jets

[1] A Biographical Notice by Mrs Reynell (privately printed).
[2] *Cambridge University Reporter*, Dec. 17, 1904.

of wittiness at the least provocation, caring for things which other boys did not care for, misliking the classics, especially Greek, but "brought out by Chaucer" as his tutor Mr E. D. Stone reports, and discovering some taste for mathematics and a passionate interest in music. One contemporary remembers his "jolly, curiously-lined face"; another writes that he was regarded as "a thoroughly good fellow," but his striking originality of mind was perhaps only realised by one schoolfellow, Gerald Balfour, who was the sharer of many a Sunday walk and both at Eton and Cambridge bound to Maitland by close ties of friendship. To the masters Maitland presented none of the obvious points of interest. Even William Johnson, that learned and catholic scholar who made so many happy discoveries, failed to discover Maitland. The boy was not a Hellenist and his deficiencies in Greek and Latin prosody put him outside the intellectual pale. He was whimsical, full of eccentric interests, of puns and paradox and original humour. His closest school friend thought that he would possibly develop into "a kind of philosophic Charles Lamb[1]."

In the autumn of 1869 Maitland went up to Trinity College, Cambridge, as a Commoner. The learned Samuel Roffey had been a musician both in theory and practice, and the taste for music descended through the son to the grandson. The first year of Maitland's undergraduate life was given over to music, mathematics and athletics; but his earliest distinctions were

---

[1] A punning squib, very spirited and amusing, entitled "A solemn Mystery," and contributed to *The Adventurer*, June 4, 1869, seems to have been Maitland's first appearance in print.

gained not in the most but in the least intellectual of these pursuits. Though he can never have looked otherwise than fragile, he had outgrown his early delicacy and become an active lad with considerable powers of endurance. He won the Freshman's mile in four minutes forty-seven seconds, excellent time as records went then, and obtained his "blue" as a three-miler in the Inter-University Sports. The two mile walking race, the quarter, and the mile, fell to him at various times in the Third Trinity Sports. Nor were his athletic activities confined to the running path. His friend Mr Cyprian Williams remembers his last appearance as a racing oarsman; how on the final day of the Lent races of 1872 the Third Trinity second boat after a successful week made a crowning bump, how in the moment of the victory the crew were tipped over into the cold and dirty waters of the Cam, and how in the evening the boat dined in Maitland's lodgings over Palmer's bootshop and kept up its festivity well into the morning.

Long before this—at the beginning of his second year at Cambridge—Maitland found his way into Henry Sidgwick's lecture-room and made a discovery which shall be told in his own words. " It is now thirty years ago that some chance—I think it was the idle whim of an idle undergraduate—took me to Sidgwick's lecture-room, there to find teaching the like of which had never come in my way before. There is very much else to be said of Sidgwick; some part of it has been beautifully said this afternoon; but I should like to add this: I believe that he was a supremely great teacher. In the first place I remember the admirable patience which could never be out-worn by stupidity, and which nothing but pretentiousness could disturb. Then there was the sympathetic and kindly endeavour to overcome our shyness, to make us talk, and to make us think. Then there was that marked dislike for any mere reproduction of his own opinions which made it impossible for Sidgwick to be in the bad sense the founder of a school. I sometimes think that the one and only prejudice that Sidgwick had was a prejudice against his own results. All this was far more impressive and far more inspiriting to us than any dogmatism could have been. Then the freest and boldest thinking was set forth in words which seemed to carry candour and sobriety and circumspection to their furthest limit. It has been said already this afternoon, but I will say it again : I believe that no more truthful man than Sidgwick ever lived. I am speaking of a rare intellectual virtue. However small the class might be, Sidgwick always gave us his very best; not what might be good enough for undergraduates, or what might serve for temporary purposes, but the complex truth just as he saw it, with all those reservations and qualifications, exceptions and distinctions which suggested themselves to a mind that was indeed marvellously subtle but was showing us its wonderful power simply because, even in a lecture room, it could be content with nothing less than the maximum of attainable and communicable truth. Then, as the terms went by, we came to think of lecture time as the best time we had in Cambridge ; and some of us, looking back now, can say that it was in a very true sense the best time that we have had in our lives. We turned away to other studies and pursuits, but the memories of Sidgwick's lectures lived on. The matter of the lectures, the theories and the arguments, might be forgotten; but the method remained, the spirit remained, as an ideal—an unattainable ideal, perhaps, but a model of perfect work. I know that in this matter I can speak for others; but just one word in my own case. For ten years and more I hardly saw Sidgwick. To meet him was a rare event, a rare delight. But there he always was: the critic and judge of any work that I might be doing: a master, who, however forbearing he might be towards others, always exacted from himself the utmost truthfulness of which word and thought are capable. Well, I think it no bad thing that young men should go away from Cambridge with such a master as that in their minds, even though in a given case little may come of the teaching...I can say no more. Perhaps I have already tried to say too much. We who were, we who are, Sidgwick's pupils, need no memorial of him. We cannot forget. Only in some way or another we would bear some poor testimony of our gratitude and our admiration, our reverence and our love[1]."

Such teaching was precisely calculated to ripen Maitland's unsuspected powers. The pupil was as modest, as exact, as truth-loving as the master, and possessed a quick turn for witty casuistry which was quite individual though not dissimilar to Sidgwick's own gift in the same direction. Under Sidgwick's

[1] *Cambridge University Reporter*, Dec. 7, 1900.

influence Maitland's intellect deepened and widened. The piano was ejected from the college room; the University running path knew him no more; mathematics were abandoned for philosophy with such good result that a scholarship was gained at Trinity, and that in the Moral and Mental Science Tripos of 1872 Maitland came out at the head of the First Class, bracketed with his friend W. Cunningham, who has since won high distinction in the field of economic history. But the chief prize of undergraduate ambition, a Fellowship at Trinity, was denied him. Maitland competed, and was beaten in the competition by James Ward, now one of the most distinguished of living psychologists. Examiners make fewer mistakes than is commonly supposed, and on this occasion Henry Sidgwick and Thomas Fowler reached their decision not without hesitation. While admitting Maitland's literary brilliance and facility they discovered in his successful rival a deeper interest in the problems of philosophy and therefore a superior claim to a Fellowship in Moral and Mental Science[1].

Maitland's Fellowship dissertation entitled "A Historical Sketch of Liberty and Equality as Ideals of English Political Philosophy from the time of Hobbes to the time of Coleridge" is, despite some defects of proportion, a remarkable performance for so young a man. Not only does it cover a wide range

---

[1] There were four candidates for the Fellowship: W. Cunningham, Arthur Lyttelton, F. W. Maitland, and James Ward, every one of them distinguished in after life. With so strong a competition the College might have done well to elect more Fellows than one in Moral and Mental Science.

of reading, especially in the English moralists, but it is distinguished by two characteristic qualities—independence of judgment and a scrupulous estimate of the canons of proof. The scholar of Trinity says many good things[1], but says nothing at random. Even when it would have been tempting to sally forth with a flourish of affirmation, he prefers to stand within the zone of caution. "I am inclined to think," he writes, "(though there is great risk of such speculations being wrong) that Hobbes was led to exaggerate his account of man's naturally unsocial character by a desire to bring the state of nature into discredit." One cannot dogmatise about the motives of the dead; our dogmas are but plausible hypotheses, and so complex is human nature, so inexhaustible is life's casuistry that the likeliest conjecture may fail of the mark. "There is a great risk of such speculation being wrong." Touches like this reveal the fact that the disciple of Sidgwick had learnt his master's lesson.

The scholarship at Trinity, carrying with it a place at the scholar's table, brought Maitland into communion with the ablest men in the College. It often happens that a youth who has attracted little attention at school

---

[1] Such for instance as :—

"The love of simplicity has done vast harm to English Political Philosophy."

"No history of the British Constitution would be complete which did not point out how much its growth has been affected by ideas derived from Aristotle."

"The idea of a social compact did not become really active till it was allied with the doctrine that all men are equal."

"In Hume we see the first beginnings of a scientific use of History."

by reason of his failure to satisfy the limited conventions of schoolboy excellence, springs into sudden prominence at the University. His conversation attracts notice; his friends discover that he has original opinions, or some peculiar charm of bearing, or that his gifts of mind or character are out of the common. So it was with Maitland. He soon achieved a reputation not only as a witty and brilliant talker, but as a charming companion and as the most original public speaker of his time. He was elected to be a member of the Apostles, a small society which for many university generations has been a bond between clever young Cambridge men and has brought them into friendly relations with their seniors: and by the suffrages of a larger and less select electorate he rose to be Secretary and then President of the Union Society.

Maitland's speeches at the Union printed themselves upon the minds of his audience as being very effective for their immediate purpose and yet quite unlike the speeches of ordinary vote-winners. His artifice was all his own. Others were more eloquent, more prompt in the cut and thrust of debate, but in the power of condensing an argument into a surprising phrase or epigram he stood alone. After his first successful appearance as the advocate of the opening of National Collections of Science and Art on Sunday afternoons he became the favourite undergraduate orator of his time. "You insist that we must keep the Mosaic Law," he argued in his maiden speech, "but under it a man who gathered sticks on the Sabbath was stoned to death. Now I have picked up sticks on Sundays. Will you in your consistency stone me?"

On another occasion he delighted the House by observing that at the Reformation the English State put an end to its Roman bride but married its deceased wife's sister. The shape of his opinions was frankly radical and fashioned by a vehement enthusiasm for free thinking and plain speaking. " There are two things," he remarked, " which we have learnt by costly experience that the Law cannot control—Religious Belief and the Rate of Interest." Compulsory attendance at College Chapel, Church Establishment, the closing of the Cambridge Union on Sunday mornings aroused his opposition and furnished the theme of well-remembered speeches. " O Sir," he once exclaimed to the President with outstretched hands, " I would I were a vested nuisance ! Then I should be sure of being protected by the whole British Public."

There is a pleasant story contributed by Professor Kenny—to whom this portion of the narrative is greatly indebted—of a debate upon a motion that certain annotations upon the annual report of the Union's proceedings should be cancelled in the interests of " the literary credit of the Society." The notes were ungrammatical, ludicrous, unauthorised. They had been composed during the Long Vacation by the Society's senior servant in the name of the absent Secretary. There was nothing to be said for them save that it was hard that a good old man should be humiliated for an excess of official zeal. Maitland was Secretary at the time and chivalrously undertook the defence of his subordinate. It was the eve of the Fifth of November ; the name of the mover was

James. Such an historical coincidence was not lost upon the ingenious mind of the Secretary. "To-morrow," he observed, boldly carrying the war into the enemy's country, "is the Feast of the Blessed Saint Guy. Appropriately enough the House appears to be under search this evening for indications of a new plot. Enter King James the Third, surrounded by his minions, with a loud flourish of his own trumpet. He produces the dark lantern of his intellect and discovers—not a conspirator, but a mare's nest." And when, at last, by successive strokes of humour Maitland had won over the sympathies of the House, he proceeded to venture upon the merits of his defence. "We are attacked," he said, "for bad grammar. A great crime, no doubt, in some men's eyes. For at times I have met men to whom words were everything, and whose everything was words ; men undistinguished by any other capacity, and unknown outside this House, but reigning here in self-satisfaction, lords of the realm of Tautology."

II.

The failure to obtain a fellowship broke off any design which may have been entertained of an academic career, and Maitland, following the family example, returned to London to try his fortune at the bar. Men of high academic achievement sometimes fail in the practical professions, by reason of a certain abstract habit of mind or from an engrained unsociability of temperament. Neither of these disadvantages affected Maitland. A combined training in philosophy and law had given him just that capacity for deriving principles from the facts of experience, and of using the facts of experience as the touchstone of principles, which is essential to the adroit and intelligent use of legal science ; and for all his learning and zeal there was nothing harsh and unsocial about him. On the other hand he was completely deficient in the moral alloy which appears to be an essential element in the fabric of most successful careers. He was entirely destitute of the arts of "push" or advertisement, and so disinterested and self-effacing that a world which is accustomed to take men at their own valuation was not likely to seize his measure.

Maitland entered at Lincoln's Inn in 1872 and was called to the bar in 1876, reading first with Mr Upton and afterwards with Mr B. B. Rogers, the brilliant translator and editor of Aristophanes. "I had only one vacancy," writes Mr Rogers, "in my pupil room and that was about to be filled by a very distinguished young Cambridge scholar. But he was anxious— stipulated I think—that I should also take his friend Maitland. I did not much like doing so, for I considered four pupils as many as I could properly take, and I knew nothing of Maitland and supposed that he would prove the crude and awkward person that a new pupil usually is, however capable he may be, and however distinguished he may become in later life. However, I agreed to take him as a fifth pupil, and he had not been with me a week before I found that I had in my chambers such a lawyer as I had never met before. I have forgotten, if I ever knew, where and how he acquired his mastery of law; he certainly did not acquire it in my chambers: he was a consummate lawyer when he entered them. Every opinion that he gave was a complete legal essay, starting from first principles, showing how the question agreed with one, and disagreed with another, series of decisions and finally coming to a conclusion with the clearest grasp of legal points and the utmost lucidity of expression. I may add (and though this is a small point it is of importance in a barrister's chambers) that it was given in a handwriting which it was always a pleasure to read. He must have left me in 1877, and towards the end of 1879, my health being in a somewhat precarious state, and my medical advisers insisting orí my lessening the strain of my work, I at once asked Maitland to come in and superintend my business. He gave up his own chambers and took a seat in mine (the chambers in 3 Stone Buildings where I then was are I think the largest in the Inn), superintended the whole of my business, managed my pupils, saw my clients and in case of necessity held my briefs in Court. I doubt if he would have succeeded as a barrister; all the time that I knew him he was the most retiring and diffident man I ever knew; not the least shy or awkward; his manners were always easy and self-possessed; but he was the last man to put himself forward in any way. But his opinions, had he suddenly been made a judge, would have been an honour to the Bench. One of them may still be read in Re Cope Law Rep. 16 Ch. D. 49. There a long and learned argument filling nearly two pages of the Report is put into the mouth of Chitty Q.C. and myself, *not one word of which was ever spoken by either of us.* It was an opinion of Maitland's on the case laid before us which I gave to Chitty to assist him in his argument....I cannot close this long though hastily written letter without expressing my personal esteem for the man. Wholly without conceit or affectation, simple, generous and courteous to everybody, he was the pleasantest companion that anybody could ever wish for: and I think that the three years he spent in my chambers were the most delightful three years I ever spent at the bar."

Working partly for Mr Rogers and partly for Mr Bradley Dyne, Maitland saw a good deal of conveyancing business and in after years was wont to lay stress upon the value of this part of his education. Conveyancing is a fine art, full of delicate technicalities, and Maitland used to say that there could be no better introduction to the study of ancient diplomata than a few years spent in the chambers of a busy conveyancer. Here every document was made to yield up its secret; every word and phrase was important, and the habit of balancing the precise practical consequences of seemingly indifferent and conventional formulæ became engrained in the mind. Paleography might teach men to read documents, diplomatics to date them and to test their authenticity; but the full significance of an ancient deed might easily escape the most exact paleographer and the most accomplished diplomatist, for the want of that finished sense for legal technicality which is the natural fruit of a conveyancing practice.[1]

[1] For a good instance of Maitland's trained insight see *Domesday Book and Beyond*, p. 232.

Business of this type, however, does not provide opportunities for forensic oratory and Maitland's voice was rarely heard in Court[1]. But meanwhile he was rapidly exploring the vast province of legal science, mastering the Statute Books, reading Frenchmen, Germans and Americans, and occasionally contributing articles upon philosophical and legal topics to the Press.

To the deepest and most serious minds the literature of knowledge is also the literature of power. Maitland's outlook and ideal were at the period of intellectual virility greatly affected by two books, Savigny's *Geschichte des Römischen Rechts* and Stubbs' *Constitutional History*. The English book he found in a London Club and "read it because it was interesting," falling perhaps, as he afterwards suggested, for that very reason "more completely under its domination than those who have passed through schools of history are likely to fall." Of the German he used to say that Savigny first opened his eyes as to the way in which law should be regarded.

> Justinian's Pandects only make precise
> What simply sparkled in men's eyes before,
> Twitched in their brow or quivered in their lip,
> Waited the speech that called but would not come[2].

Law was a product of human life, the expression of human needs, the declaration of the social will; and so a rational view of law would be won only from some height whence it would be possible to survey the great

[1] Maitland once conducted an argument before Jessel, M. R. Re Morton v. Hallett (Feb. & May, 1880, Ch. 15, D. 143).

[2] Browning, *Ring and the Book*. See Maitland, *Bracton's Note Book*, vol. I.

historic prospect which stretches from the Twelve Tables and the *Leges Barbarorum* to the German Civil Code and the judgments reported in the morning newspaper. Readers of *Bracton's Note Book* will remember Maitland's description of Azo as "the Savigny of the thirteenth century," as a principal source from which our greatest medieval jurist obtained a rational conception of the domain of law. Savigny did not write the same kind of book as Azo. He worked in a different medium and on a larger canvas but with analogous effects. He made the principles of legal development intelligible by exhibiting them in the vast framework of medieval Latin and Teutonic civilization and as part of the organic growth of the Western nations. Maitland's early enthusiasm for the German master took a characteristic form: he began a translation of the history.

The translation of Savigny was neither completed nor published. Maitland's first contribution to legal literature was an anonymous article which appeared in the *Westminster Review* in 1879. This was not primarily an historical disquisition though it displayed a width of historical knowledge surprising in so young a man, but a bold, eloquent, and humorous plea for a sweeping change in the English law of Real Property. "Let all Property be personal property. Abolish the heir at law." This alteration in the law of inheritance would lead to great simplification and would remove much ambiguity, injustice and cost. Nothing short of this would do anything worth doing. A few little changes had been made in the past, "for accidents will happen in the best regulated museums," but it was no use recommending timid subsidiary changes while the central anomaly, the source of all complexity and confusion, was permitted to continue. "It is not unlikely," remarked the author with grave irony, "that we are behind an age whose chief ambition is to be behind itself."

The article exhibits a quality of mind which is worth attention. Maitland never allowed his clear strong common sense to be influenced by that vague emotion which the conventional imagination of half-informed people readily draws from antiquity. He loved the past but never defended an institution because it was old. He saw antiquity too vividly for that. And so despite the ever increasing span of his knowledge he retained to the end the alert temper of a reformer, ready to consider every change upon its merits, and impelled by a natural proclivity of mind to desire a state of society in some important respects very different from that which he found existing. At the same time he is far too subtle a reasoner to acquiesce in the doctrinaire logic of Natural Rights or in some expositions of social philosophy which pretended to refinements superior to those provided by empirical utilitarianism. Two early articles contributed to the pages of *Mind* on Mr Herbert Spencer's *Theory of Society* contain a modest but very sufficient exposure of the shortcomings of that popular philosopher's *a priori* reasoning in politics.

With these serious pursuits there was mingled a great deal of pleasant recreation. Holidays were spent in adventurous walking and climbing in the Tyrol, in Switzerland, and among the rolling fir-clad hills of the

Black Forest, for Maitland as a young man was a swift and enduring walker, with the true mountaineer's contempt for high roads and level places. We hear of boating expeditions on the Thames, of visits to burlesques and pantomimes, of amusing legal squibs and parodies poured out to order without any appearance of effort. From childhood upwards music had played a large part in Maitland's life and now that the shadow of the Tripos was removed he was able to gratify his musical taste to the full. In 1873 he spent some time alone in Munich, listening to opera night after night and then travelled to Bonn that he might join his sisters at the Schumann Commemoration. Those were the days when the star of Richard Wagner was fast rising above the horizon and though he was not prepared to burn all his incense at one shrine, Maitland was a good Wagnerian. In London musical taste was experiencing a revival, the origin of which dated back, perhaps, to the starting of the Saturday Concerts at the Crystal Palace by August Manns in 1855. The musical world made pilgrimages to the Crystal Palace to listen to the orchestral compositions of Schubert and Schumann or to the St James' Hall popular concerts, founded in 1859, to enjoy the best chamber music of the greatest composers. New developments followed, the first series of the Richter Concerts in 1876 and the first performance of Wagner's *Ring* in 1882. Maitland with his friend Cyprian Williams regularly attended concert and opera. Without claiming to be an expert he had a good knowledge of music and a deep delight in it. One of his chief Cambridge friends, Edmund Gurney, best known perhaps as one of the principal founders of the Society for Psychical Research, wrote a valuable book on *The Power of Sound* and interested Maitland in the philosophy of their favourite art. "I walked once with E. Gurney in the Tyrol," Maitland wrote long afterwards, "What moods he had! On a good day it was a joy to hear him laugh!" Gurney died prematurely in 1888 and the increasing stress of work came more and more between Maitland and the concert room; but problems of sound continued to exercise a certain fascination over his mind and his last paper contributed to the Eranos Club at Cambridge on May 8, 1906, and entitled with characteristic directness "Do Birds Sing?" was a speculation as to the conditions under which articulate sound passes into music.

That by the natural workings of his enthusiastic genius Maitland would have been drawn to history whatever might have been the outward circumstances of his career, is as certain as anything can be in the realm of psychological conjecture. Men of the ordinary fibre are confronted by alternatives which are all the more real and painful by reason of their essential indifference. This career is open to them or that career, and they can adapt themselves with equal comfort to either. But the man of genius follows his star. His life acquires a unity of purpose which stands out in contrast to the confused and blurred strivings of lesser men. Other things he might do, other tastes he might gratify; but there is one thing that he can do supremely well, one taste which becomes a passion, which swallows up all other impulses, and for which he is prepared to sacrifice money and health and the pleasures of society and many other things which are prized among men.

When Maitland stood for the Trinity Fellowship he was already aware that success at the bar would mean the surrender of the reading which had "become very dear" to him, and yet his ambition desired success of one kind or another. The varied humours of his profession pleased him; he loved the law and all its ways; yet it is difficult to believe that the routine of a prosperous equity business would ever have satisfied so comprehensive and enquiring a mind. The young barrister had a soul for something beyond drafts; he lectured on political economy and political philosophy in manufacturing towns and in London[1], wrote for the *Pall Mall Gazette*, then a liberal evening paper under the direction of Mr John Morley; but more and more he was drawn to feel the fascination and importance of legal history. Two friends helped to determine his course. Mr, now Sir Frederick, Pollock had preceded Maitland by six years at Eton and Trinity and was also a member of Lincoln's Inn. Coming of a famous legal family, and himself already rising to distinction as a scientific lawyer, Mr Pollock appreciated both the value of English legal history and the neglect into which it had been allowed to fall. He sought out Maitland and a friendship was formed between the two

---

[1] An account of Maitland's "valuable" lectures "On the Cause of High and Low Wages," given to an average class of some twenty workmen in the Artizan's Institute, Upper St Martin's Lane, in 1874, and "followed by a very useful discussion in which the students asked and Mr Maitland answered many knotty questions" may be read in H. Solly, *These Eighty Years*, vol. II. p. 440.

men which lasted in unbroken intimacy and frequent
intellectual communion to the end. An historical note
on the classification of the Forms of Personal Action,
contributed to his friend's book on the *Law of Torts*,
was the first overt evidence of the alliance.

The other friend was a Russian. Professor Paul
Vinogradoff, of Moscow, who had received his historical education in Mommsen's Seminar in Berlin,
happened in 1884 to be paying a visit in England.
The Russian scholar, his superb instinct for history
fortified by the advantages of a system of training
such as no British University could offer, had, in
a brief visit to London, learnt something about the
resources of our Public Record Office which was
hidden from the Inns of Court and from the lecture
rooms of Oxford and Cambridge. On January 20,
Maitland and Vinogradoff chanced to meet upon one
of Leslie Stephen's Sunday tramps, concerning which
there will be some words hereafter, and at once discovered a communion of tastes. The two men found
that they were working side by side and brushing one
another in their researches. Correspondence followed
of a learned kind ; then on Sunday, May 11, there was
a decisive meeting at Oxford. The day was fine and
the two scholars strolled into the Parks, and lying full
length on the grass took up the thread of their historical discourse. Maitland has spoken to me of that
Sunday talk ; how from the lips of a foreigner he first
received a full consciousness of that matchless collection
of documents for the legal and social history of the
middle ages, which England had continuously preserved
and consistently neglected, of an unbroken stream of

authentic testimony flowing for seven hundred years, of tons of plea-rolls from which it would be possible to restore an image of long-vanished life with a degree of fidelity which could never be won from chronicles and professed histories. His vivid mind was instantly made up: on the following day he returned to London, drove to the Record Office, and being a Gloucester-shire man and the inheritor of some pleasant acres in that fruitful shire asked for the earliest plea-roll of the County of Gloucester. He was supplied with a roll for the year 1221, and without any formal training in paleography proceeded to puzzle it out and to tran-scribe it.

The *Pleas of the Crown for the County of Glou-cester* which appeared in 1884 with a dedication to Paul Vinogradoff is a slim and outwardly insignificant volume; but it marks an epoch in the history of history. "What is here transcribed," observes the editor, "is so much of the record of the Gloucester-shire eyre of 1221 as relates to pleas of the Crown. Perhaps it may be welcome, not only to some students of English law, but also (if such a distinction be main-tainable) to some students of English history. It is a picture, or rather, since little imaginative art went to its making, a photograph of English life as it was early in the thirteenth century, and a photograph taken from a point of view at which chroniclers too seldom place themselves. What is there visible in the fore-ground is crime, and crime of a vulgar kind—murder and rape and robbery. This would be worth seeing even were there no more to be seen, for crime is a fact of which history must take note; but the political life of England is in a near background. We have here, as it were, a section of the body politic which shows just those most vital parts, of which, because they were deep-seated, the soul politic was hardly conscious, the system of local government and police, the organization of county, hundred, and township."

It was the publication of a new and fundamental type of authority accomplished with affectionate and exquisite diligence by a scholar who had a keen eye for the large issues as well as for the minutiæ of the text. And it came at a timely moment. Sir James Fitzjames Stephen's *History of Criminal Law* had recently appeared and Maitland has written of it in terms of genuine admiration ; but remarkable as those volumes undoubtedly were, miraculous even, if regard be paid to the competing claims upon the author's powers, they did not pretend to extend the boundaries of medieval knowledge. The task of making discoveries in the field of English legal antiquity, of utilizing the material which had been brought to light by the Record Commission appeared to have devolved upon Germans and Americans. All the really important books were foreign—Brunner's *Schwurgerichte*, Bigelow's *Placita Anglo-Normannica* and *History of Procedure in England*, the *Harvard Essays on Anglo-Saxon Law*, Holmes' brilliant volume on the *Common Law*. Of one great name indeed England could boast. Sir Henry Maine's luminous and comprehensive genius had drawn from the evidence of early law a number of brilliant and fascinating conclusions respecting the life and development of primitive society, and had applied an intellectual impulse which made itself felt in every branch of serious historical enquiry. But the very seductions of Maine's method, the breadth of treatment, the all-prevailing atmosphere of nimble speculation, the copious use of analogy and comparison, the finish and elasticity of the style were likely to lead to ambitious and ill-founded imitations. It is so pleasant to build theories ; so painful to discover facts. Maitland was strong enough to resist the temptation to premature theorizing about the beginnings of human society. As an undergraduate he had seen that simplicity had been the great enemy of English Political Philosophy ; and as a mature student he came to discover how confused and indistinct were the thoughts of our forefathers, and how complex their social arrangements. What those thoughts and arrangements were he determined to discover, by exploring the sources published and unpublished for English legal history. He knew exactly what required to be done, and gallantly faced long hours of unremunerative drudgery in the sure and exultant faith that the end was worth the labour. "Everything which he touched turned to gold." He took up task after task, never resting, never hasting, and each task was done in the right way and in the right order. The study of English legal history was revolutionised by his toil.

Before the fateful meeting with Vinogradoff at Oxford, Maitland had made friends with Leslie Stephen. In 1880 he joined "the goodly company, fellowship or brotherhood of the Sunday tramps," which had been founded in the previous year by Stephen, George Crome Robertson, the Editor of

Mind, and Frederick Pollock. "The original members of the Society about ten in number were for the most part addicted to philosophy, but there was no examination, test, oath or subscription, and in course of time most professions and most interests were represented." The rule of the Club was "to walk every other Sunday for about eight months in the year," and so long as Maitland lived in London he was a faithful member of that strenuous company. A certain wet Sunday lived in his memory and, though he did not know it, lived also in the memory of Leslie Stephen. "I was the only tramp who had obeyed the writ of summons, which took the form of a postcard. When the guide (we had no 'president,' certainly no chairman, only so to speak, a 'preambulator') and his one follower arrived at Harrow station, the weather was so bad that there was nothing for it but to walk back to London in drenching rain; but that day, faithful alone among the faithless found, I learnt something of Stephen, and now I bless the downpour which kept less virtuous men indoors." That wet Sunday made Maitland a welcome guest at the Stephen's house; and it brought other happiness in its train. In 1886 Maitland was married in the village church of Brockenhurst, Hants, to Florence Henrietta, eldest daughter of Mr Herbert Fisher, some time Vice Warden of the Stannaries, and niece of Mrs Leslie Stephen. Two daughters, the elder born in 1887, and the younger in 1889, were the offspring of the marriage.

III.

Meanwhile Maitland had been recalled from London to his old University. The reading which had been "very dear to him" when he took the first plunge into London work, had become dearer in proportion as the opportunities for indulging in it became more restricted. He was earning an income at the bar which, though not large, was adequate to his needs, but a barrister's income is uncertain and Maitland may have felt that while he had no assured prospect of improving his position at the bar, the life of a successful barrister, if ever success were to come to him, would entail an intellectual sacrifice which he was not prepared to face. Accordingly in 1883 he offered himself for a Readership in English Law in the University of Oxford, but without success. A distinguished Oxford man happened to be in the field and the choice of the electors fell, not unnaturally, upon the home-bred scholar. But meanwhile a movement was on foot in the University of Cambridge to found a Readership in English Law. In a Report upon the needs of the University issued in June, 1883, the General Board of Studies had included in an appendix a statement from the Board of Legal Studies urging that two additional teachers in English Law should be established as assistants to the Downing Professor. Nothing however was done and the execution of the project might have been indefinitely postponed but for the generosity of Professor Henry Sidgwick, who offered to pay

£300 a year from his own stipend for four years if a Readership could be established. Sidgwick's action was clearly dictated by a general view of the educational needs of the University, but he had never lost sight of his old pupil and no doubt realised that Maitland was available and that he was not unlikely to be elected. The Senate accepted the generous offer, the Readership was established, and on November 24, 1884, Maitland was elected to be Reader of English Law in the University of Cambridge. In the Lent term of 1885 he gave his first course of lectures on the English Law of Contracts.

Cambridge offered opportunities for study such as Maitland had not yet enjoyed. A little volume on Justice and Police, contributed to the English Citizen series and designed to interest the general reading public, came out in 1885, and affords good evidence of Maitland's firm grasp of the Statute book and of his easy command of historical perspective. But this book, excellent as it is, did not represent the deeper and more original side of Maitland's activity any more than an admirable series of lectures upon Constitutional History which were greatly appreciated by undergraduate audiences but never published in his lifetime. The Reader in English Law was by no means satisfied with providing excellent lectures covering the whole field of English Constitutional history, though he had much that was fresh and true to say about the Statutes of the eighteenth century and about the degree to which the theories of Blackstone were applicable to modern conditions, and though he drew a picture for his undergraduate audience which in some important respects was closer to fact than Walter Bagehot's famous sketch of the English Constitution published while Maitland was an Eton boy. Text book and Lectures were but interludes in the main operations of the campaign against the unconquered fastnesses of medieval law. First came a remarkable series of articles contributed to the *Law Quarterly Review* upon the medieval doctrine of seisin which Maitland's sure insight had discerned to be the central feature in the land law of the Norman and Angevin period: and then in 1887 Bracton's Note Book.

"Twice in the history of England has an Englishman had the motive, the courage, the power to write a great readable reasonable book about English Law as a whole." The task which William Blackstone achieved in the middle of the eighteenth century, Henry de Bratton, a judge of the King's Court, accomplished in the reign of Henry III. His elaborate but uncompleted treatise *De Legibus et Consuetudinibus Angliæ*, composed in the period which lies between the legal reforms of Henry II. and the great outburst of Edwardian legislation, while the Common law of England was still plastic and baronage and people were claiming from the King a stricter observance of the great Charter, is naturally the most important single authority for our medieval legal history. Though influenced by the categories and scientific spirit of Roman Law, Henry de Bratton was essentially English, essentially practical. His book was based upon the case law of his own age—
Et sciendum est quod materia est facta et casus qui

quotidie emergunt et eveniunt in regno Angliæ—and
especially upon the plea-rolls of two contemporary
judges, Walter Raleigh and William Pateshull. An
edition in six volumes executed for the Rolls Series
by Sir Travers Twiss had been completed in 1883,
the year before Maitland paid his first visit to the
Record Office and discovered the plea-rolls of the
County of Gloucester ; but the text was faulty and far
from creditable to English scholarship.

On July 19, 1884, Professor Vinogradoff, "who in
a few weeks" wrote Maitland, "learned, as it seems
to me, more about Bracton's text than any Englishman
has known since Selden died," published a letter in
the *Athenæum* drawing attention to a manuscript in
the British Museum, which contained " a careful and
copious collection of cases " for the first twenty-four
years of Henry III., a collection valuable in any case,
since many of the rolls from which it was copied have
long since been lost, but deriving an additional and
peculiar importance from the probability that it was
compiled for Bracton's use, annotated by his own
hand and employed as the groundwork of his treatise.
Yet, even if the connection with Bracton could not be
established, a manuscript containing no fewer than two
thousand cases from the period between 1217 and
1240 was too precious a discovery to be neglected.
Here was a mass of first-hand material, valuable alike
for the genealogist, the lawyer, the student of social
history :—glimpses of archaic usage, of local custom,
evidence of the spread of primogeniture, important
decisions affecting the status of the free man who held
villein lands, records of villein service, vivid little

fragments of family story, some of it tragic, some of it squalid, as well as passages of general historical interest, entries concerning "the partition and therefore the destruction of the Palatinate of Chester" or the reversal of the outlawing of Hubert de Burgh the great justiciar who at one time "held the kingdom of England in his hand."

The Note Book was edited by Maitland in three substantial volumes and with the lavish care of an enthusiast. An elaborate argument, all the more cogent because it is not overstrained, raised Vinogradoff's hypothesis to the level of practical certainty. "The treatise is absolutely unique ; the Note Book so far as we know is unique ; these two unique books seem to have been put together within a very few years of each other, while yet the Statute of Merton was *nova gracia* ; Bracton's choice of authorities is peculiar, distinctive ; the compiler of the Note Book made a very similar choice ; he had, for instance, just six consecutive rolls of pleas *coram rege* ; Bracton had just the same six ; two-fifths of Bracton's five hundred cases are in this book ; every tenth case in this book is cited by Bracton; some of Bracton's most out of the way arguments are found in the margin of this book... the same phrases appear in the same contexts.... Corbyn's case, Ralph Arundell's case are 'noted up' in the Note Book ; they are 'noted up' also in the Digby MS of the treatise ; with hardly an exception all the cases thus 'noted up' seem plainly to belong to Bracton's county....Lastly we find a strangely intimate agreement in error ; the history of the ordinance about special bastardy and the 'Nolumus' of

Merton is confused and perverted in the two books. Must we not say then that, until evidence be produced on the other side, Bracton is entitled to a judgment, a possessory judgment?" The penultimate argument in the pleading was characteristic of Maitland's ingenuity and also of a favourite pastime. He describes an imaginary walking tour through Devon and Cornwall and points out that ten cases noted up in the margin of the Note Book refer to persons and places which must have been well known to Bracton. "Many questions are solved by walking. *Beati omnes qui ambulant.*"

The appearance of the Note Book showed that Cambridge possessed a scholar who could edit a big medieval text with as sure a touch as Stubbs, and the book received a warm welcome from those who were entitled to judge of its merits. It had been a costly book to prepare and it was brought out at Maitland's own charges. In the introduction he took occasion to point out that in other countries important national records were apt to be published by national enterprise; and that in England the wealth of unpublished records was exceptional. "We have been embarrassed by our riches, our untold riches. The nation put its hand to the work and turned back faint-hearted. Foreigners print their records; we, it must be supposed, have too many records to be worth printing; so there they lie, these invaluable materials for the history of the English people, unread, unknown, almost untouched save by the makers of pedigrees." As an advertisement of these unknown treasures no more fortunate selection could have been made than this manuscript note book which could with so high a degree of probability be associated with the famous name of Bracton. But Maitland was not content with urging that the publication of our unknown legal records should not be left to depend upon the chance enthusiasm of isolated scholars; he demanded, as things necessary to the progress of his subject, a sound text of Bracton's treatise and a history of English Law from the thirteenth century.

In 1888 there was by reason of the death of Dr Birkbeck a vacancy in the Downing Chair of the Laws of England. Maitland stood and was elected. His Inaugural Lecture delivered in the Arts School on 13th October, 1888, was entitled, "Why the History of Law is not written." The reason was not a lack of material; on the contrary England possessed a series of records which "for continuity, catholicity, minute detail and authoritative value has—I believe that we may safely say it—no equal, no rival in the world," nor yet the difficulty of treating the material, for owing to the early centralization of justice, English history possessed a wonderful unity. Rather it was "the traditional isolation of English Law from every other study" and the fact that practising lawyers are required to know a little medieval law not as it was in the middle ages, but as interpreted by modern courts to suit modern facts. "A mixture of legal dogma and legal history is in general an unsatisfactory compound. I do not say that there are not judgments and text books which have achieved the difficult task of combining the results of deep historical research with luminous and accurate exposition of existing law—

neither confounding the dogma nor perverting the history; but the task is difficult. The lawyer must be orthodox otherwise he is no lawyer; an orthodox history seems to me à contradiction in terms. If this truth is hidden from us by current phrases about 'historical methods of legal study,' that is another reason why the history of our law is unwritten. If we try to make history the handmaid of dogma she will soon cease to be history."

Maitland concluded with an appeal for workers in an untilled field, but with characteristic veracity held out no illusory hopes. "Perhaps," he wrote, "our imaginary student is not he that should come, not the great man for the great book. To be frank with him this is probable; great historians are at least as rare as great lawyers. But short of the very greatest work, there is good work to be done of many sorts and kinds, large provinces to be reclaimed from the waste, to be settled and cultivated for the use of man. Let him at least know that within a quarter of a mile of the chambers in which he sits lies the most glorious store of material for legal history that has ever been collected in one place and it is free to all like the air and the sunlight. At least he can copy, at least he can arrange, digest, make serviceable. Not a very splendid occupation and we cannot promise him much money or much fame....He may find his reward in the work itself: one cannot promise him even that; but the work ought to be done and the great man when he comes may fling a footnote of gratitude to those who have smoothed his way, who have saved his eyes and his time."

stock or marketable securities which undoubtedly are not the
same thing as the lands and trade marks.'

Now it may occur to you that in their anxiety to
avoid a confusion of the persons our courts fall into the opposite
of error and divide the substance. But that is not so. The
old things still exist and are owned, though new things, 'transferable
in the books of the company' have come into being. Also it
seems possible that we may easily over-estimate the creative

powers of lawyers and courts and legislators. Let us remember that these new things will be things for the man of business, things for the Stock Exchange. And in passing let us ask ourselves whether if these 'things' are not unreal, the humanity of the company must needs be fictitious?

Fragment of a Lecture

As yet Maitland had not conceived himself as the author of that "History of English Law from the thirteenth century," the need for which he proclaimed to his Cambridge audience. A less extensive scheme had framed itself in his mind "some thoughts about a plan of campaign for the History of the Manor." The thoughts were communicated to Frederick Pollock and were not unfruitful, for they grew up seven years later into that massive *History of English Law* which is perhaps Maitland's most enduring title to fame; but of his learned projects in this seed-time and of some other concerns, grave and gay, a few scraps of correspondence may here most fittingly be adduced in evidence.

To Paul Vinogradoff.

6, New Square,
Lincoln's Inn.
28 *April,* 1884.

I am indeed glad that you are working at Bracton and settling the relation between the MSS. I wish that you would stay here and teach us something about our old books. Pollock is looking forward to your paper and I am diligently reading Bracton in order that I may understand it. I have written for Pollock a paper about seisin and had occasion to deal with a bit of Bracton which, as printed, is utter rubbish. I therefore looked at some of the MSS and found that the blunder was an old one. I shall not have occasion to say any more than that there are manuscripts which make good sense of the passage—but I have made a note[1] about the matter which I send to you thinking it just possible that you may care to see it, as it goes some little way (a very little way) to show that certain MSS are closely related.

I have to dine in Oxford on Saturday, 10th May, and shall be there on Sunday the 11th. I hope that you will be in Oxford on that day and that we shall meet.

To Frederick Pollock.

(On a postcard.)

Jan. 1881.

Et Fredericus de Cantebrigia essoniavit se de malo lecti, et essoniator dixit quod habuit languorem. Set quia essonium non jacet in breui de trampagio consideratum est quod summoneatur et quod sit in misericordia pro falso essonio suo. Postea uenit et defendit omnem defaltam et sursisam et dicit quod non debet ad hoc breve respondere quia non tenetur ire in trampagio nisi tantum quando dominus capitalis suus eat in persona sua propria nec vult nec debet ire cum ballivo vel preposito, et ipse et omnes antecessores sui semper a conquestu Anglie usque nunc habuerunt et habent talem libertatem, et de hoc ponit se super patriam, etc.

Revera predictus F. seisitus fuit de uno frigore valde damnando. Judicium—Recuperet se ipsum.

---

[1] The note shows a knowledge of 18 Bracton MSS.

To Frederick Pollock.

15, Brookside,
Cambridge.
12 *Nov.* 1887.

Very many thanks to you for a copy of your book on "Torts"—I am already deep in it and am reading it with delight. You will believe that coming from me this is not an empty phrase, for you will do me the justice of believing that I can find a good book of law very delightful. I hope that it may be as great a success as "Contracts"—I can hardly wish you better. I now see some prospect of getting the Law of Torts pretty well studied by the best of the undergraduates. For weeks I have been in horrible bondage to my lectures—Stephen's chapters about the Royal Prerogatives and so forth—I speak of the Stephen of the Commentaries—are a terrible struggle : when one is set to lecture on them three days a week one practically has to write a book on constitutional law against time.

I cannot, alas, be at the Selden meeting on Monday, for I have undertaken to audit some accounts.

With many more thanks I rest
Sectator tuus set minus sufficiens.

F. W. Maitland.

To Paul Vinogradoff.

15, Brookside,
Cambridge.
12 *June*, 1887.

"Cuius linguam ignorabant"—I feel now the full force of these words—I am in tenebris exterioribus, and there is stridor dencium; but I heartily congratulate you upon having finished your book[1], and thank you warmly for the copy of it that you sent me and for the kind words that you wrote upon the outside. Also I can just make out my name in the Preface and am' very proud to see it there.   Also I have read the footnotes and they are enough to show me that this is a great book, destined in course of time to turn the current of English and German learning.

My book also is finished, but the printers are slow. I hope to send you a copy in the autumn.   I have been able to add a few links to the chain of argument that you forged.   My happiest discovery was about a note that you may remember, "Ermeiard et herede de Hokesham."   I found (1) that the heir of Huxham was in ward to William of Punchardon, (2) that William's wife was Ermengard, (3) that Ermengard brought an action for her dower against Henry of Bratton.   I have also had some success with Whitchurch, Gorges, Corner and Winscot.

[1] The Russian edition of *Studies in Villeinage.*

To FREDERICK POLLOCK.

JUBILEE TEAPOT TOR,
HORRABRIDGE.
26 *July*, 1887.

Horrabridge seems to be as much our post town as any other place; but I have not fully fathomed our postal relations. The legend is that the old gentleman who squatted here—and if ever I saw an untitled squatment I see one now—held that the post was "a new found holiday" and charged the postman never to come near him—and the postman, holding this to be an acquittance for all time, refused and still refuses to visit Pu Tor, but leaves our letters somewhere, I know not where, whence they are fetched by Samuel the son of the house—which Samuel learned the first half of the alphabet in the school "to" Sumpford Spiney Church-town when as yet there was a school, but the school scattered and beyond N Samuel does not go—howbeit, there will be a school again some day if ever Mr Collier can catch A. J. Butler at the Education Office, which is hardly to be expected. But if I begin to tell the acts of the Putorians, I shall never cease, for they are a race with a history and a language and (it may be) a religion of their own. Villani de Tawystock fecerunt cariagium—but the ignorant beggars did not know Pu Tor cottage and it seemed that we should wander about all night. This is a right good spot and we are grateful to you for discovering it. We have a sitting-room and two bedrooms and we could find place for a visitor if his stomach were not high. Have you seen the new ordnance map of the moor? Mr Collier showed it me. *Pew* Tor is the spelling that it adopts.

To Frederick Pollock.

15, Brookside,
Cambridge.
7 *April*, 1888.

I have returned from a brief incursion of Devonshire. Verrall and I made a descent upon Lynton which is still beautiful and at this time of the year unbetouristed. Bank Holiday was tolerable. I suppose that you spent it upon your freehold and are now returning to the law. You have got an excellent number of the *L. Q. R.*[1] this quarter; really it ought to sell and if it doesn't the constitution of the universe wants reforming....

If P objects to "ville" as a termination for names in America what does he say to "wick" as a termination for names in England? I have been puzzling over the use of "villa" in Kemble's *Codex*. It seems to be used now for a village or township and now for a single messuage, and thus seems similarly elastic. One never can be quite certain what is meant when a villa is conveyed.

I have had some thoughts about a plan of campaign for the history of the manor. The graver question is whether the story should be told forwards or backwards. I am not at all certain whether it would not

[1] *Law Quarterly Review.*

be well to begin by describing the situation as it was at the end of cent. XIII. and then to go back to earlier times. But we can talk of this when "possession" is off your mind. Remember that you have to stay here as an examiner. Meanwhile I hope to form a provisional scheme for your consideration.

I have got hold of a German, one Inama Sternegg, who seems to be the modern authority as to the growth of the manorial system on the continent.

To Frederick Pollock.

(On a postcard.)

9 *May*, 1888.

Predicti sokemanni habebunt remedium per tale breve de Monstraverunt.

R tali duci salutem. Monstraverunt nobis N N homines de trampagio vestro quod exigis ab eis alia servicia et alias consuetudines quam facere debent et solent videlicet in operibus et ambulationibus, et ideo vobis precipimus quod predictis hominibus plenum rectum teneas in curia tua ne amplius inde clamorem audiamus, quod nisi feceris vicecomes noster faciat. Teste Meipso apud Cantebrigiam die Ascen. Dñi.

To Paul Vinogradoff.

3, Albany Terrace,
St Ives,
Cornwall.
25 *July*, 1888.

I ought before now to have sent you my address to meet the case of your having any MS to send me.

I have been going over and over again in my mind many parts of the pleasant talk that we had at Cambridge during two of the most delightful days of my life. I hope that you were not weary of instructing me. Let me say that the more I think of your theory of folk land the better I like it. Of course it is a theory that must be tested and I know that you will test it thoroughly: but it seems to me a true inspiration, capable of explaining so very much, and I think that it will be for English readers one of the most striking things in your book. Should you care for notes on any of the following matters I can send them to you out of my Selden materials—(1) persons with surname of "le Freman" paying merchet, (2) free men refuse to serve on manorial jury, (3) the lord makes an exchange with the Communa Villanorum, (4) persons who pay merchet on an ancient demesne manor use the little writ of right.

To FREDERICK POLLOCK.

3, ALBANY TERRACE,
ST IVES,
CORNWALL.
5 *Aug.* 1888.

Many thanks for your telegram: it was kind of you to send so prompt a message[1]. I feel it a little absurd that I should be thanking you for the telegram and no more—but I must be decorous. However, let us put the case that in a public capacity you regret the

---

[1] Announcing Maitland's election to the Downing Chair.

result, still it is allowed me to think that in the capacity of friend you rejoice with me and of course I am very happy. I wonder whether you dined in Downing. I hope that my essoin was taken in good part ; but really I thought that there would be an insolent confidence apparent in my journeying from St Ives to Cambridge in order to be present at a dinner. It might, I think, have been reasonably said that I did not come all that way to grace the triumph of another man....Well, I am glad that I have ceased to regard you as my judge and can resume unrestrained conversation.

To Frederick Pollock.

3, Albany Terrace,
St Ives,
Cornwall.
6 *Aug.* 1888.

Your letter from Downing tells me what I expected, namely, that the struggle was severe. I can very well understand that there was much to be said against me —some part of it at all events I have said to myself day by day for the last month. My own belief to the last moment was that some Q.C. who was losing health or practice would ask for the place and get it. As it is, I am reflecting that in spite of all complaints the bar at large must still be doing a pretty profitable trade, otherwise this post would not have gone begging.

To Paul Vinogradoff.

22, Hyde Park Gate, S.W.
September, 1888.

Has this occurred to you?—how extremely different the whole fate of English land law would have been if the King's court had not opened its doors to the under-vassals, to the lowest freeholders. But this was a startling interference with feudal justice and only compassed by degrees, in particular by remedies which in theory were but possessory etc. Now if the lower freehold tenants had not had the assizes, the line between them and the villein tenants would have been far less sharp. You hint at all this in chap. IV but might it not be worth a few more words—for there will be a tendency among your readers to say *of course* freeholders had remedies in the King's courts while really there is no of course in the matter. The point that I should like emphasized—but perhaps you are coming to this—is that not having remedies in the King's own court is not equivalent to not having rights.

Downing.
14 *Oct.* 1888.

I have been picking up my strength and am doing a little work. Yesterday I got through my inaugural lecture; possibly I may print it and in that case I will ask you to accept a copy; but it was meant to be heard and not read and so I allowed myself some exaggerations.

...I am now quite ready to see proofs of your book....My Introduction for the manorial rolls is taking shape; it will deal only with the courts, their powers and procedure. You can I think trust me not to take an unfair advantage of our correspondence and your kindness—but if you had rather that I did not see the sheets of your book which deal with the courts, please say so. I hope to have got this Introduction written in a month or six weeks.

To Henry Sidgwick.

THE WEST LODGE,
DOWNING COLLEGE,
CAMBRIDGE.
11 *Dec.* 1888.

I have been reading your proof sheets[1] with great interest, and really as regards the parts which most concern me I have little to suggest. I think the chapter on law and morality particularly good. Were I writing the book I should in my present state of ignorance "hedge" a little about continental notions of law. Since I had some talk with you I have been reading several German law books, and my view of the duties of a German judge is all the more hazy. I find that a jurist, even when he is writing about elementary legal ideas, e.g. possession, will cite "Entscheidungen der oberste Gerichte von Celle, Darmstadt, Rostock etc., *if he thinks them sound*—but how far he would think himself bound as judge by

---

[1] Professor Sidgwick's *Elements of Politics* was published in 1891.

decisions which made against his theory I cannot tell. All seems rendered so vague by the notion of a heutige römische Recht. But I think that you have just hit off the English idea of a good judge—he does *justice* when he sees an opportunity of doing it. I do not think that a man could be a judge of quite the highest order without a strong feeling for political morality. On p. 92, chap. XII. you might add if you could do so that our highest courts of appeal, House of Lords and Judicial Committee, hold themselves bound by their own decisions in earlier cases.

As regards the existence of different laws in different parts of a country you might reckon among the advantages the gain in experience. I have no doubt that Scotch experience has improved English law and English experience Scotch law. Thus some use of an experimental method is made possible; e.g. take "Sunday closing" we can experiment on Wales and Cornwall. On the whole I have been surprised to find how little harm is done by the difference between Scotch and English law. I have read but very few cases that were caused by such differences.

I admire the chapter on International Law and Morality; it is the best thing that I have read about the subject. In my view the great difficulty in obtaining a body of international rules deserving the name of law lies in the extreme fewness of the "persons" subject to that law and the infrequency and restricted range of the arguable questions which arise between them. The "code" of actually observed rules is thus all shreds and patches. In short, international law is so incoherent.

To Paul Vinogradoff.

20 *Feb.* 1889.

You ask me about the Preface[1]—well I think it grand work, and on the whole I think it will attract readers because of its very strangeness; but you will let me say that it will seem strange to English readers, this attempt to connect the development of historical study with the course of politics; and it leads you into what will be thought paradoxes; e.g. it so happens that our leading "village communists" Stubbs and Maine are men of the most conservative type while Seebohm who is to mark conservative reaction is a thorough liberal. I am not speaking of votes at the polling booth but of radical and essential habits of mind. I think that you hardly allow enough for a queer twist of the English mind which would make me guess that the English believer in "free village communities" would very probably be a conservative— I don't mean a Tory or an aristocrat, but a conservative. On the other hand with us the man who has the most splendid hopes for the masses is very likely to see in the past nothing but the domination of the classes—of course this is no universal truth—but it comes in as a disturbing element.

---

[1] Of the English edition of Vinogradoff's *Studies in Villainage.*

To Paul Vinogradoff.

The West Lodge.
12 *March*, 1889.

Your long letter was very welcome. When I wrote I must have been in a bad temper and after I had written I wished to recall my letter. But now I no longer regret what has brought from you so pleasant an answer. Really I have no fear at all about the success of your book, if I had I would expatriate myself. But it stands thus :—Introductions are of "critical importance," by which I mean that they are óf importance to critics, being often the only parts of a book which casual reviewers care to read. As a matter of prudence therefore I put into an Introduction a passage about the book which I mean critics to copy, and they catch the bait—it saves them trouble and mistakes. But your "philosophy of history," I mean philosophy of historiography, will not lend itself to such ready treatment and may give occasion to remarks as obvious and as foolish as mine were. But I hope for better things. All that you say about Stubbs and Seebohm and Maine is, I dare say, very true if you regard them as European, not merely English, phenomena and attribute to them a widespread significance —and doubtless it is very well that Englishmen should see this—still looking at England only and our insular ways of thinking I see Stubbs and Maine as two pillars of conservatism, while as to Seebohm I think that his book is as utterly devoid of political importance, as, shall I say Madox's *History of the Exchequer*? But you are cosmopolitan and I doubt not that you are right. You are putting things in a new light—that is all—if "the darkness comprehendeth it not," that is the darkness's fault. And now as to Essay I. I have nothing to withdraw or to qualify. I think it superb, by far the greatest thing done for English legal history. I am looking forward with the utmost anxiety to Essay II.

To Paul Vinogradoff.

Downing.

15 *Nov.* 1891.

Even the title page has been passed for the press and I am now awaiting your book. I shall be proud when I paste into you the piece of paper that you sent me. I have felt it a great honour to correct your proof sheet and am almost as curious about what the critics will say as if the book were my own. I often think what an extraordinary piece of luck for me it was that you and I met upon a "Sunday tramp." That day determined the rest of my life. And now the Council of the University has offered me the honour of doctor "honoris causa." I was stunned by the offer for it is an unusual one and of course I must accept it. But for that Sunday tramp this would not have been. As to the reception of your book my own impression is that it will be very well received. Good criticism you can hardly expect, for very few people here will be able to judge of your work. But I think that you will be loudly praised. Perhaps you will become an idol like Maine—who can tell? I hardly wish you this fate, though you might like it for a fortnight. I was ill in September, but am better now and have been doing a good many things—preparing myself for some paragraphs about Canon law.

IV.

The year which brought Maitland to Downing witnessed the appearance of a new volume from his pen entitled *Select Pleas of the Crown* 1200–1255. It was a handsome quarto, bound in dark blue cloth, and the first publication of a Society called after the name of John Selden. The Selden Society, planned in the autumn of 1886 and founded in the following year " to encourage the study and advance the knowledge of English law," was the creature of Maitland's enthusiasm, and of all his achievements stood nearest to his heart. Indeed, without disparagement to accomplished help-mates and contributors, it may be said that without Maitland's genius, learning and devotion the Selden Society would have been unthinkable. Eight of the twenty-one volumes issued by the Society during his lifetime came from his pen ; a ninth was almost completed at his death. " Of the rest every sheet passed under his supervision either in manuscript or in proof, and often in both[1]." He set the standard, planned the

---

[1] " Frederick William Maitland," by B. F. L., *Solicitor's Journal*, Jan. 5, 1907. See also *The Year Books of Edward II* (Selden Society), vol. IV., Preface.

programme, trained many of the contributors. It is difficult to recall an instance in the annals of English scholarship in which so large an undertaking has owed so much to the diligence and genius of a single man.

Both in conception and execution it is a noble series of volumes. Maitland's interest in law was not bounded by a province, a period, or a country; and the thirteen good and lawful men who on November 24, 1886, signed the letter from which the Selden Society sprang did not make their appeal to the Bar and Bench of England in the cause of any narrow or pedantic antiquarian curiosity. The Common law of England ruled two vast continents, and was the concern of Americans, Canadians, and Australians as well as of Englishmen and Irishmen. Its history had never been written; few of the materials for its exploration had been given to the world. There was no scientific grammar or glossary of the Anglo-French language; there was no accurate dictionary of law terms; a great province, that of Anglo-Saxon law, had fallen into the occupation of the Germans. A short account of some of the principal classes of Records which might be dealt with by the Society was appended to the first two volumes and exhibited a prospect of great breadth, richness and variety. The state of the Criminal law in early times might be shown from the Eyre rolls and Assize rolls. The records of the Court of the Exchequer and the Court of Chancery, the Privy Council Registers, the proceedings before the Starchamber, the Court of Requests and the Court of Augmentations would illustrate the history of royal justice in its different sides and in different ages, in the formative period of legal and parliamentary growth, in the dreary turmoil of Lancastrian anarchy, under the vigorous despotism of the Tudors and in the dust of the great conflict which led to the Civil War. Then there were the records of the Courts Christian, of the Courts of the Forest and the Manor, records illustrating the history of the Palatine jurisdictions, the franchises of the Lords Marchers of Wales, the Court of the Staple in London and Calais, the Court of Castle Chamber in Dublin. Borough customs would throw light on one quarter of history; records of the Stanneries of Devon and Cornwall upon another. The origins of mercantile and international law might be explored; and closer knowledge could be obtained of many important State trials by a systematic account of the contents of the *Baga de Secretis.* The Society held out the further hope of scientific contributions to the knowledge of the Anglo-Saxon law and Anglo-French language of the Year Books.

In the selection of specimens from this copious material, Maitland displayed a felicitous strategy the aim of which was to exhibit, as rapidly as might be, the range and versatility of the Society's operations. A sequence of volumes illustrating any one department of law would fatigue attention, warn off subscribers and fail to make the desired impression on the general historical public. It was better to begin upon several different types of record than to work one vein without intermission; better for the cause of science, and a course more likely to bring forward good contributors as well as to stimulate public interest in the undertaking. With a general editor less perfectly equipped such a scheme might have been hazardous; but Maitland was master of the whole field and could be trusted not to fail in proportion and perspective. In swift succession the members of the Selden Society received volumes illustrating Pleas of the Crown, Pleas of Manorial Courts, Civil Pleas, manorial formularies, the Leet jurisdiction of Norwich, Admiralty Pleas; then an edition of the *Mirror of Justice* followed by a volume on *Bracton and Azo*. Of these first eight volumes Maitland wrote four and contributed a brilliant introduction to a fifth—the edition of the *Mirror*, executed by his pupil and friend Mr W. J. Whittaker. It was an astonishing performance; even had the work been spread over twelve years of robust energy it would still have been astonishing. It was accomplished in half that time by a busy, delicate, University Professor who apart from statutory Professorial lectures was simultaneously engaged in writing the classical *History of English Law.*

Much might be said by qualified persons as to the exquisite technique displayed in Maitland's contributions to the Selden Society. He spared no pains in the examination and collation of manuscripts, and although he modestly disdained expert paleographical knowledge, he need not, we imagine, fear comparison with the most accurate transcribers of medieval documents, or with those who have achieved a special renown for their studies in "diplomatic" or in the affiliation of manuscripts. He possessed other qualities which are not often combined with such a passion and gift for minute scholarship. In the first place he was exceedingly anxious to make his work practically useful and to ease the path for students whose tastes might lead them to attempt similar explorations. He takes the reader into his laboratory and exhibits the whole process of discovery, showing where the difficulties lie, pointing out hopeful lines of enquiry, and providing always a clear chart to the documents, published and unpublished, of his subject. Secondly he combined in an extraordinary measure the gift for hypothesis with the quality of patience. He did not aim at providing sensational or curious results ;—"the editor," he writes in the introduction to the first Selden volume, "has not conceived it his duty to hunt for curiosities, the history of law is not a history of curiosities"—he wished for plain truth—to discover the course of medieval justice in all its natural and instructive monotony, in its common forms and in its everyday working garb. "It has been necessary," he writes, referring to his selection of manorial pleas, "to print some matter which in itself is dull and monotonous ; a book full of curiosities would be a very unfair representative of what went on in the local courts. We cannot form a true notion of them unless we know how they did their ordinary work, and this we cannot know until we have mastered their common forms." Such a scheme no doubt involves repetition, but there is at least one student of English history who, despite some acquaintance with histories and chronicles, never understood the everyday working of medieval life until he had the good fortune to dive into the publications of the Selden Society.

A saying used to be attributed to E. A. Freeman

to the effect that it is impossible to write history from manuscripts ; and it is obvious that a man who uses manuscript authority to any great extent, especially if he imposes upon himself great labours of transcription, will run the risk of losing his perspective and will be inclined to attach undue importance to those parts of his evidence which have cost him most sacrifice to obtain. On the other hand it is clear that the editor of historical manuscripts will do his work much better if he is also an historian ; and this is specially true if he is called upon to pick and choose out of a vast repository of unedited material those specimens which are most likely to promote the advance of scientific knowledge. Maitland brought to the task of editing legal records an exact and comprehensive knowledge of the various problems, each in its proper order of importance, towards the solution of which his material might be expected to contribute. Like a skilful advocate examining a string of reluctant witnesses he had in his mind a provisional scheme of the whole transaction to quicken and define his curiosity. "These rolls," he writes, "are taciturn, they do not easily yield up their testimony, but must be examined and cross-examined." It was a close, seductive, patient cross-examination, one in which a little matter would often suggest an important conclusion, as where it is shown that the rapid development of the Common law in the thirteenth century is mirrored on the surface of the plea-rolls, which become fuller, more regular and more mechanical as the century goes on. And this cross-examination being conducted with great subtlety, vividness and penetration resulted in substantial discoveries. Each volume contributed new thought as well as new facts. The preface to *Select Pleas of the Crown* traced the gradual differentiation of the several branches of the Royal Court in the early part of the thirteenth century and embodied valuable conclusions "drawn from a superficial perusal of all the rolls of John's reign" as to the state of criminal justice and criminal procedure at that epoch. The Introduction to the *Select Pleas of Manorial Courts* was even more important, giving as it did for the first time an account of the stages in the decline of the English private courts and supplying an analysis, subtler than any which had yet been attempted, of the legal connotation of the term "manerium" and of the composition of the manorial courts. One suggestion was startling in its originality. The orthodox theory, contained in the works of Coke, had laid it down that a Court Baron could not be held without at least two freeholders. Maitland came upon the whole to the conclusion—though he is careful to state countervailing arguments—that originally no distinction was made between the freeholders and customary tenants. Both classes attended the Manorial Court and both classes gave judgment. Distinctions, however, did come to be drawn, and this by reason of a force the operation of which had escaped the notice of enquirers who had not been trained to attend to legal phenomena—by the force of legal procedure. "New modes of procedure are emphasising distinctions which have heretofore been less felt. The freehold suitors can maintain their position[1], the customary suitors

[1] I.e. as Domesmen.

become mere presenters and jurymen with the lord's steward as their judge. Every extension of royal justice at the expense of feudal does some immediate harm to the villein. It is just because all other people can sue for their lands and their goods in the King's own Court that he seems so utterly defenceless against the lord : 'the custom of the manor' looks so like 'the will of the lord' just because the humblest freeholder has something much better than the custom of the manor to rely upon, for he has the assizes of our lord the King, the Statutes of King and Parliament."

The third volume edited by Maitland for the Selden Society consisted of two parts—a collection of Precedences for use in seignorial and other local courts belonging to the thirteenth and early part of the fourteenth century, and Select Pleas from the Bishop of Ely's Court at Littleport. Here there was less matter for elaborate historical disquisition, for the main problem with regard to the first class of document was to settle the age of the manuscripts ; but the brief introduction to the Littleport pleas contained an im-portant suggestion with regard to the early history of the English law of Contract. Were not the local courts enforcing "formless" arguments long before the King's Court had developed the action of "assumpsit" for the enforcement of agreements not under seal ? The reader is reminded that the King's Court never by any formal act or declaration took upon itself to enforce the whole law of the land, that only by degrees did its "catalogue of the forms of action become the one standard of English law." There was an action for defamation in the local courts long before the

King's Court had undertaken to punish the slanderer;
and what was true of defamation might equally be true
of "parol" agreements. The Bishop's Court at Littleport was certainly enforcing agreements and it was
difficult to suppose that the villeins of Littleport put
their contracts into writing. Here again a few slight
indications had prompted a secure and far-reaching
inference.

In the *Institutes* of the learned but uncritical Coke
there are many tales drawn from a curious Anglo-
French treatise entitled the *Mirror of Justices*, "a very
ancient and learned treatise of the laws and usages of
this kingdom," opined Sir Edward, "whereby the
Common-wealth of our nation was governed about
eleven hundred years past." For a long time the book
was accepted at Coke's high valuation with no little
injury to the sober study of legal antiquities. Then it
was exposed as apocryphal by Sir Francis Palgrave.
It could not be taken as evidence "concerning the early
jurisprudence of Anglo-Saxon England." But could
it be taken as evidence of anything at all? *Wahrheit
und Dichtung* was Vinogradoff's verdict,—sediments
of truth floating in a sea of absurdity. It was worth
while at least to establish the text and to examine
the credentials of a treatise which, like the pseudo-
Ingulph, had done much harm to sound learning.

One reassuring result was obtained from Mr
Whittaker's critical enquiry into the manuscript. The
Mirror was never in the middle ages a popular
or influential book. It existed in a single unique
manuscript. Such authority as it obtained was conferred upon it by lawyers who lived some three

hundred years after it was written, were "greedy of old tales and not too critical of the source from which they were derived." Still, in a book so full of concrete positive statement, so full of denunciation of practical abuses, there might for all its rubble of absurdity be a quarry for historians.

In a brilliant piece of persiflage Maitland once and for all demolishes the author of the *Mirror*. He exposes his wilful lies, his unctuous piety, the perverse originality which amuses itself by playing havoc among technical terms, his absence of all lawyerly interest, his perplexing and fantastic inconsistencies. A most ingenious hypothesis is advanced to explain the source of this curious piece of apocryphal literature. "In order to discover the date of its composition we ask what statutes are, and what are not, noticed in it, and we are thus led to the years between 1285 and 1290. Then we see that its main and ever-recurring theme is a denunciation of 'false judges,' and we call to mind the shameful events of 1289. The truth was bad enough ; no doubt it was made far worse by suspicions and rumours. Wherever English men met they were talking of 'false judges' and the punishment that awaited them. All confidence in the official oracles of the law had vanished. Any man's word about the law might be believed if he spoke in the tones of a prophet or apostle. Was not there an opening here for a fanciful young man ambitious of literary fame ? Was not this an occasion for a squib, a skit, a topical medley, a 'variety entertainment,' blended of truth and falsehood, in which Bracton's staid jurisprudence should be mingled with freaks and

crotchets and myths and marvels, and decorated with
queer tags of out-of-the-way learning picked up in the
consistories?" No doubt, as Maitland admitted, this
was guess-work; the certainty was that no statement
not elsewhere warranted could be accepted from the
Mirror unless we were prepared to believe "that an
Englishman called Nolling was indicted for a sacrifice
to Mahomet."

V.

The Chair of the Laws of England carried with it
a Fellowship and an official house at Downing. The
College, standing apart from "the sights" of Cambridge
and possessing neither antiquarian nor architectural
interest, is probably neglected even by the most
conscientious of our foreign visitors. Yet during
Maitland's tenure of the Downing Chair distinguished
jurists from many distant parts, from America, Germany,
Austria, France, found their way "through the incon-
spicuous gateway opening off the main business street"
into the spacious quadrangle, with its pleasant grove
of lime and elm, and its two rows of late Georgian
buildings fronting one another across the grass. One
of these guests has recorded his impressions. "About
the middle of the row on the western side Maitland
had his house. His study was a plain square room,
not entirely given up to law or history and not over-
crowded with folios. Yet every book on the shelves
had evidently been chosen; there was no useless
pedantic lumber. One gained at once an impression

of refined taste and sure critical judgment. The work-shop mirrored the worker. The view from the study window was that of the open lawn and the monotonous row of houses opposite. But on the western side the house was set right into the thicket. Here every sort of English songster seemed to have its nest[1]."

Maitland at least was well content. He loved Cambridge, every stone of it, and prized its friend-ships. There were Henry Sidgwick, his old master in philosophy; and A. W. Verrall, an exact equal in University standing, who had become intimate with him at Trinity, had shared his chambers at Lincoln's Inn but had abandoned the law for the Greek and Latin Classics; there were C. S. Kenny, a friend of undergraduate days, a Union orator and a criminal lawyer; and G. W. Prothero, who bore most of the weight of the historical teaching in the University; and Henry Jackson, who long afterwards succeeded Jebb in the Chair of Greek; and R. T. Wright, the Secretary to the University Press. For Dr Alex Hill, the Master of Downing, Maitland soon came to entertain feelings of affectionate admiration. Nor was his power of making friends limited to men of his own age. His directness of manner, his simplicity and humour at once secured him the confidence and respect of younger men, and he rapidly made his name as one of the most inspiring teachers in the University, giving to the student, in Mr Whittaker's eloquent words, "a sense of the im-portance, of the magnificence, of the splendour of the study in which he was engaged, so that it was impossible at any time thereafter for one of his pupils to regard

---

[1] *Political Science Quarterly*, vol. XXII., No. 2, p. 287.

the law merely as a means of livelihood[1]." His method
of lecturing, like everything else he did, was quite
individual. The lecture was carefully written and read
in a slow distinct impressive voice to the audience, so
slowly that it was possible to take very full notes, and
yet with such a rare intensity of feeling in every word
and intonation, with such quiet and unsuspected jets of
humour, such electric flashes of vision, that the hearers
were never weary, and one of them has reported
that Maitland made you feel that the history of law in
the twelfth century was the only thing in life worth
living for. Stories, too, have reached the sister University of witty speeches made after dinner, as for
instance on November 11, 1897, when fourteen of Her
Majesty's judges were entertained in the Hall of
Downing upon the occasion of the Lord Chief Justice
receiving an honorary degree, and the speech of the
evening was made by the Professor of the Laws of
England. And there were other less august occasions.
The members of a distinguished and occult society
record a series of impromptu speculations as to the
character of the company assembled round the table.
Were they the Salvation Army? No, they were not
musical. Were they the Board of Works? Were
they the Saved of Faith?—and so on through a series
of hypotheses each more grotesque and fantastic than
the last and delivered in the clear grave tones which
made Maitland's humour irresistible.

Among the most welcome guests at Brookside in
the days of the Readership and at the West Lodge in
the early days of Maitland's tenure of the Downing

[1] *Cambridge University Reporter*, July 22, 1907, p. 1313.

Chair was J. K. Stephen, the brilliant author of *Lapsus Calami.* J. K. Stephen, son of Sir James and nephew of Leslie Stephen, most tender, witty, and vivacious of companions, was on every account dear to Maitland and his wife.

In January, 1888, Stephen launched a weekly magazine called *The Reflector.* It was the year in which Maitland exchanged Brookside for Downing, the year of the first publication of the Selden Society, and finally the year of Mr Ritchie's County Council Act. Being invited to contribute a paper to the new periodical Maitland chose as his theme the impending revolution in English local government. The administrative functions of the Justices of the Peace were to be transferred to elective County Councils. In a charming essay full of ripe wisdom and pleasant wit Maitland bade farewell to the old order and expressed some of the misgivings which the inevitable change aroused in his mind. Master Shallow and Master Silence were to be stripped of half their functions and might come to the conclusion that the other half was not worth preserving. That which was "perhaps the most distinctively English part of all our institutions," the Commission of the Peace, was attacked in a vital part, not because the Justices had been corrupt or extravagant, but because the spirit of the age condemned them. "The average Justice of the Peace is a far more capable man than the average alderman, or the average guardian of the poor; consequently he requires much less official supervision. As a governor he is doomed; but there has been no accusation. He is cheap, he is pure, he is capable, but he is doomed; he is to be sacrificed to a theory, on the altar of the spirit of the age." Regrets, however, were vain. On the contrary, since the control of the central Government was already vested in the people, it was best that the people should gain political experience in local affairs, that the local authorities should be given a free hand to manage and to mismanage, and that care should be taken to invest them with such a degree of dignity and independence as should attract the best men into the public service. Maitland did not often express himself on public affairs; but he watched them closely and took no conclusions at second-hand.

It is part of our English system to expect of our professors, however eminent they may be, that they should examine undergraduates, serve on boards, committees, syndicates, and take an active part in University and College affairs. Maitland did not seek to escape any duty which he might be expected to discharge. He examined five times in the Law Tripos, twice in the Historical Tripos and three times in the Moral Science Tripos. From November, 1886, to January, 1895, he served as secretary to the Law Board, and always took an active share in its work. He was a member of the Library Syndicate (helping to redraft its regulations), he served on the General Board of Studies, and in 1894 was elected to the Council of the Senate. Nobody is so valuable on a committee as a good draftsman and Maitland's quick and exact draftsmanship caused his services to be highly esteemed by any board or syndicate of which he was a member. "He took," says Mr Wright, "little part in the discussions of these bodies unless he

had something definite to say, but was always ready to
state his views on being appealed to, and it is not
necessary to say that they always carried great weight."
The Dean of Westminster, who for some time sat next
to him at the Council meetings, was impressed by the
"sagacity and courage" of his judgments in the interpretation of statutes. "'I always stretch a statute,' he
whispered to me once half humourously. He seemed
to be making the law grow under his hands[1]."

In the public debates of the Senate House he was
rarely heard, but when he spoke there was a sensation.
Academic oratory is generally above the average in
tone and ability, but is seldom spirited or passionate,
and often goes astray into subtleties and side issues.
In the judgment of some members of his audience,
Maitland's speaking was quite unlike any other oratory
which was heard in Cambridge. The whole man
seemed quick with fire. His animation was so intense
that it hardly seemed to belong to a northern temperament, expressing itself with dramatic force in every
line of his eloquent face, in every movement of hand
and arm and in the rhythm of the body which swayed
with the spoken word. The language of his speeches,
which had been carefully thought out, was clear and
weighty, full of pungent humour and unexpected turns,
and stamped with the impress of a restrained but
vehement idealism. The speech on Women's Degrees
was a masterpiece after its kind and very little was
heard of a proposal to establish a separate University
for Women after Maitland had suggested that it should
be called the "Bletchley Junction Academy"—"for

[1] *Cambridge University Reporter*, June 22, 1907, p. 1303.

at Bletchley you change either for Oxford or for Cambridge."

The oration against compulsory Greek, though less cogent in substance, was hardly less striking in form.

College business claimed and received no small part of the time which under the system of the continental Universities would have been devoted to the advancement of knowledge. "When," writes Dr Hill, "in 1888 Maitland was elected Downing Professor of the Laws of England, the older members of the Society, knowing his attachment to Trinity, doubted whether he would feel himself naturalised in the smaller College. From the moment of his admission all misgivings vanished. With characteristic chivalry he assumed and almost over-acted his new *rôle*. His eager patriotism was a challenge to our own. He was prepared to out-do Downing men in his labours in all matters pertaining to the welfare of the College." If a Statute was to be interpreted, if title deeds were to be scheduled, if a voyage was to be made to the Record office in search of "feet of fines," Maitland was at hand willing and eager to interpret, to schedule, to investigate. "In all questions of interpretation," Dr Hill continues, "Maitland was standing counsel to the College as he was to the University." It so happened that when he joined Downing rents were rapidly falling and that the management of the estates entailed much care and thought. College meetings were very frequent and not a few of the special difficulties which arose, involved legal proceedings. Maitland, who for three years received no part of his salary as fellow, put himself unreservedly at the disposition of the College, and an academic society struggling to extricate itself from financial embarrassments could not have invoked a more valuable ally. Now he would help to draft a memorial to the Master of the Rolls; now a bill to be brought before Parliament. " His legal training and knowledge and his nicely balanced judgment were of inestimable use in the solution of the special problems with which the College had to deal." But it was not in legal matters only that he gave service without stint. " He was equally loyal in taking his share in all phases of administration and in doing all that in him lay to enrich the College life. He dined regularly in Hall and spent the evening in the combination room to the delight of his own guests and those introduced by other members of the Society." The Master of Downing might be painting the portrait of an ideal Fellow; those who know the College best will be the last to dispute its resemblance.

In the summer of 1892 Maitland advertised a course of lectures upon "Some Principles of Equity," and from that date onward till 1906 a course upon equity—" Equity more especially Trusts " was the favourite title—figured in the yearly programme of the Downing Professor. At first the subject was packed into the Lent term; then the lectures grew and overflowed into the summer. " I put in some business," he would observe gaily, "the business" consisting of recent decisions of the Chancery division, for the lectures were revised year by year to keep pace with the march of knowledge and the requirements of the practical student. Of these discourses there is the less reason to speak, even if the present writer were entitled to be heard, seeing that they have now been given to the world, thanks to the labour of two distinguished and devoted pupils. Maitland explained to his audience the whole system of modern equity, and when a lawyer is unfolding the Administration of Assets or the doctrines of Conversion, Election and Specific Performance to qualified persons, the layman would do well to keep his peace. It is, however, a quality in Maitland that much as he enjoyed the technicalities of law, he was never content to be purely technical. The same gifts which shone out in his conversation, the genius for perspicuous and graphic description, the quick darting flight to the essential point, the fertile power of exhibiting a subject in new and original aspects were conspicuous in his handling of the least promising topics, and these lectures could never have been written by a man who was nothing more than a sound Chancery practitioner. What is equity and what is its relation to the common law? So simple and fundamental do these questions appear to be that one would imagine that the correct answer to them must have been given again and again. It is one of those numerous cases in which a truth which appears to be quite obvious as soon as it is pointed out has lain if not unperceived, at least imperfectly perceived, because the proper perspective depends upon an unusual combination of studies. Maitland, doubly equipped as an historian and a lawyer, found no difficulty in demonstrating two propositions which had never been clearly stated before, first that "equity without common law would have been a castle in the air and an impossibility," and second "that we ought to think of the relation between common law and equity not as that between two conflicting systems but as that between code and supplement, that between text and gloss." Such observations will soon savour of platitude. That equity was not a self-sufficient system, that it was hardly a system at all but rather "a collection of additional rules," that if the common law had been abolished equity must have disappeared also, for it presupposed a great body of common law, that normally the relation between equity and law has not been one of conflict, for the presence of two conflicting systems of law would have been destructive of all good government—such propositions only require to be stated to meet with acceptance. Yet it was left to Maitland to state them. The need for thus emphasising the essential unity of English law was due partly to the tendency of teachers to lay stress upon the cases in which there is a variance between the rules of common law and the rules of equity and partly to the fact that in the routine of his profession the practitioner would have his attention directed rather to such occasions of variance than to the necessary and intricate dependence of equity on common law. Perhaps there is no greater proof of originality than the discovery of truths, which have no surprising quality about them except the length of time during which they have gone unnoticed or obscured.

VI.

Among the operations which belong to that wonderful period of activity which culminated in the *History of English Law,* two remain to be singled out, the first an enquiry of great delicacy and of crucial importance for the history of legal procedure, the second lying somewhat outside the ordinary sphere of Maitland's investigations but of great moment to the student of parliamentary institutions. We allude to the articles upon the "Register of Original Writs" contributed to the *Harvard Law Review* in 1889 and to the *Memoranda de Parliamento* edited for the Rolls Series in 1893.

The Register of the wryttes orygynall and judiciall was first printed by William Rastell in 1531. "In its final form when it gets into print it is an organic book....To ask for its date would be like asking for the date of one of our great cathedrals. In age after age bishop after bishop has left his mark upon the church; in age after age chancellor after chancellor has left his mark upon the Register....To ask for the date of the Register is like asking for the date of English law." Yet this vast and important repertory had never been made the subject of critical examination. No one had examined the principles upon which the printed book was constructed; no one had gone behind the printed book to the manuscripts; no one had traced the life history of the organism, had fixed the chronological sequence of the successive styles in the cathedral. Yet until such critical work had been accomplished the history of the extension of royal justice and of the growth of English legal procedure could not be written in detail. Maitland's treatment of the problem is one of the most beautiful specimens of his workmanship.

He first discovers the principles of classification in the printed book; then turning to the manuscripts—and there are at least nineteen in the Cambridge University Library, over all of which he has cast his eye,—reports that no two manuscripts are alike, but that "gradually by comparing many manuscripts we may be able to form some notion of the order in which and the times at which the various writs became recognised members of the *Corpus Brevium*." Tests are then laid down by which the age of a Register may be determined, and finally we have "a few remarks about the early history of the Register" which are entirely original and of high importance. The two earliest manuscripts are examined, the MS Register of 1227 in the British Museum with its fifty-six writs, the MS Cambridge Register belonging likewise to the early part of Henry III's reign with its fifty-eight writs; and means are thus supplied for measuring the growth of law during the important period—the period of the Great Charter—which had elapsed between Glanvill's treatise and the third decade of the thirteenth century. Then we are guided through the later and more voluminous manuscripts. We are introduced to a Register with one hundred and twenty-one writs from the middle of the thirteenth century, to an Edwardian Register which contains four hundred and seventy-one writs; we see the writ of trespass taking a permanent place in the *Corpus*

Brevium under Edward II, we trace activity under Edward III and Richard II and then a slackening. By the turn of the fourteenth century the "great cathedral" is practically complete and the Register has assumed a form not substantially different from that which was printed in the reign of Henry VIII.

Maitland's contribution to parliamentary history consisted in the editing of the *Parliament Roll* for 1305. Of the vivid and picturesque interest of the petitions printed in that volume much might be written, for nowhere else can we gain so full and comprehensive a notion of the miscellaneous trans-actions and aspirations which came under the purview of a Parliament in the very early stages of its exist-. ence. But apart from this the volume is important as, furnishing a closer and more accurate view of the evolution of parliament than had previously been obtainable. All readers of Stubbs' *Constitutional History* are familiar with "the model Parliament of 1295." We are accustomed to think of that date as marking an epoch at which government by a Parliament of Three Estates is definitely secured, and as, in a certain sense, the close of the formative period of parliamentary institutions. It is true that Parliament is not yet divided into Lords and Commons, and that procedure by Bill is in the distant future. Still we have been wont to regard a Parliament as being throughout the fourteenth century a definite well-recognised institution, distinct from the King's Council and implying the presence of representatives from shire and borough. Maitland's preface to the *Memoranda de Parliamento* showed that such an impression should be modified. Ten years after the Model Parliament practice and nomenclature were still fluid. There was no distinction between Parliament and Council; the word *Parliamentum* is never found in the nominative; any solemn session of the King's Council might be termed a Parliament. The business too, transacted at these great inquests, was for the most part administrative and judicial, conducted through the examination and endorsement of petitions. At the beginning of the fourteenth century, despite the exploits of the English Justinian, we were still far from a legislature composed of the Three Estates.

Meanwhile, in a profusion of articles, Maitland was correcting old mistakes and throwing out pregnant suggestions in many departments of legal theory. The principal ideas which are to be found not only in his work upon the *History of Law* but in his subsequent speculations on Corporateness and Communalism were already in his mind during the early days of work at Downing. In his lectures on Constitutional History, delivered in 1888, he gave a description of English medieval land-tenure which substantially corresponds to the more complete exposition of the *History* in 1895, and had already hit upon that comparison between the course of feudal land-law in England and Germany, which runs, a brilliant shaft of illumination, through his whole treatment of the subject. In Bracton's explanation that the rector of a parish church is debarred from a writ of right his keen eye had detected, as early as 1891, "the nascent law about corporations aggregate and corporations sole."

He had already begun to apply dissolvent legal tests to "our easy talk of village communities." The English village, he remarked in 1892, "owns no land, and, according to our common law, it is incapable of owning land. It never definitely attained to a juristic personality." The village community of the picturesque easy-going antiquarian, who, fascinated by Maine's beautiful generalisations, was ready to find traces of archaic communism in every quarter, only reminded him of the remark in Scott's *Antiquary* "Pretorian here Pretorian there I mind the bigging o't." In two weighty articles contributed to the *Law Quarterly Review* in 1893 upon the subject of Archaic Communities, Maitland pricked some antiquarian bubbles with delicious dexterity and threw out a suggestion that the formula of development should be "neither from communalism to individualism" nor yet "from individualism to communalism" but from "the vague to the definite." In common with Hegel he believed that the world process consisted in the development of the spirit of reason becoming more and more articulate with every fresh discrimination of the intellect.

By amazing industry and a most rigid economy of time Maitland had combined with his professional duties and with the publication of several volumes of unprinted matter the composition of an elaborate treatise upon medieval law. The *History of English Law up to the time of Edward I* appeared in 1895. The work had been planned in conjunction with Maitland's old friend, Sir Frederick Pollock, was revised in common with him and issued under their joint names; but as Sir Frederick explained in a note appended to the Preface "by far the greater share of the execution" both in respect of the writing and the research belonged to Maitland. The book at once took rank as a classic. In range and quality of knowledge it invited comparison with the monumental achievement of Stubbs; and though it was necessarily of a highly technical character, the style was so easy and lucid that persons previously unversed in the technicalities of medieval, or indeed of modern, law, were able to read it with enjoyment.

The greater portion of the book deals advisedly with a comparatively limited period,—the age which lies between 1154 and 1272. "It is a luminous age throwing light on both past and future. It is an age of good books, the time of Glanvill and Richard FitzNeal, of Bracton and Matthew Paris, an age whose wealth of cartularies, manorial surveys and plea-rolls has of recent years been in part, though only in part, laid open before us in print. Its law is more easily studied than the law of a later time, when no lawyer wrote a treatise, and when the judicial records had grown to so unwieldy a bulk that we can hardly hope that much will ever be known about them. The Year Books—more especially in their present disgraceful plight—must be very dark to us if we cannot go behind them and learn something about the growth of those 'forms of action' which the fourteenth century inherited as the framework of its law. And if the age of Glanvill and Bracton throws light forward, it throws light backward also. Our one hope of interpreting the *Leges Henrici*, that almost unique memorial of the really feudal stage of legal history, our one hope of coercing Domesday Book to deliver up its hoarded secrets, our one hope of making an Anglo-Saxon land-book mean something definite, seems to lie in an effort to understand the law of the Angevin time as though we ourselves lived in it."

Perhaps the most distinct impression which the reader derives from the study of Maitland's work in the *History* is that he " seemed to understand the law of the Angevin time as though he himself lived in it." We feel that, if he had been going circuit with Walter Raleigh or William Pateshull, his learned brethren would have had little or nothing to tell him which he did not already know. The case law of the twelfth and thirteenth centuries—so far as it has survived in plea-rolls or chronicles or legal collections—was part of the familiar furniture of his mind. He knew it all and enjoyed it all in every one of its facets human and lawyerly. And with this he combined a remarkable capacity for appreciating the general tone and colour of legal thinking in that remote age. If the thinking was fluid and indistinct, Maitland would not attempt to make it clearer or more consistent than it really was. The vagueness would be analysed and measured. The opaque thought would be exhibited in its fluctuating and conflicting subconscious elements. We are always being reminded of that wise saying in the Fellowship Dissertation, that English political philosophy has suffered by overmuch simplicity.

A mind so exact and disinterested and endowed with so rare a capacity for divesting itself of the intellectual accretions of its own age was naturally full of dissolvents for ambitious theories. Maitland expressed in his Inaugural lecture his high respect for the genius and learning of Henry Maine, and nothing which was then written would have been afterwards retracted. Yet the close study of English medieval law had brought him to the conclusion that some of the generalisations to which Maine seemed disposed to assign a general validity, at least for the Indo-Germanic races, received no adequate support from the English evidence. In a brilliant discussion of the antiquities of inheritance he argues that in the present state of the evidence it would be rash to accept " family ownership," or in other words a strong form of birth-right, as an institution which once prevailed among the English in England. Maine, operating chiefly with Roman law but also drawing upon Teutonic, Slavonic and even Indian evidence, had argued that the primitive unit of society was an agnatic patriarchal group and that the ownership of land was vested in a family or clan constructed on strict agnatic principles and governed by the pater-familias. Maitland submits the conception of common ownership to analysis. Common ownership implies corporate ownership, and the idea of a corporation is modern, not primitive. Co-ownership indeed there was, but co-ownership spells individualism. If there is a law which declares how shares should be distri-buted among the members of the group upon partition, then there is a law which assigns ideal shares in the unpartitioned land. There was no proof that anything which ought to be called family-ownership existed among the Anglo-Saxons; there was no proof of the patriarchal *gens*, of the agnatic group. On the contrary there was a grave difficulty in accepting the patriarchal family as the primitive unit of English society, for the earliest rules about Anglo-Saxon inheritance and the Anglo-Saxon blood-feud exhibit the fact that "the persons who must bear the feud and who may share the weregild are partly related through the father and partly through the mother." Birth-rights indeed there were, but birth-rights do not imply agnation or corporate ownership. In some cases they may even be the consequence of intestate succession. Submitted to concrete tests of this character the evidence for the strict agnatic land-owning group in England became in Maitland's eyes very ghostly[1]. "In Agnation," wrote Maine, "is to be sought the explanation of that extraordinary rule of English law which prohibited brothers of the half-blood from succeeding to one another's lands." Maitland's solution of "this extraordinary rule" is very different and highly characteristic of his concrete, practical turn of mind. In his opinion it is "neither a very ancient nor a very deep-seated phenomenon." He points out that the problem of dealing with the half-blood must always be difficult, and the solution is always likely to be capricious. "The lawyers of the thirteenth and fourteenth centuries had no definite solution, and we strongly suspect that the rule that was ultimately established had its origin in a few precedents."…"Our rule was one eminently favourable to the King; it gave him escheats; we are not sure

---

[1] Maitland was probably drawn too far on the path of scepticism. See Vinogradoff, *Growth of the Manor*, pp. 135–40, and Brunner, *Deutsche Rechtsgeschichte*, 2nd ed., vol. I., pp. 110 ff.

that any profounder explanation of it would be true."

In Maitland's hands a treatise upon antiquarian law became something greater than an antiquarian treatise. It became a contribution to the general history of human society. Even the most superficial reader must be struck by the number of foreign books quoted in the footnotes and by the way in which analogues and contrasts from French and German law are brought in to illustrate the course of our legal history. English law became insular; pursued a course of its own. We avoided torture; we escaped the secret and inquisitorial procedure of the continent; we developed the jury; primogeniture became the general rule among us in case of intestacy; the *retrait lignager* of the French customs did not become established in our land-law. But just for this reason it was the more necessary to understand the main stream of continental development. Many a rule which, if considered from a purely insular standpoint, might seem part of the natural order, would assume its true character of a deviation from the normal, if viewed in the larger context of European law; many features of our law apparently arbitrary would in that larger context receive explanation. Maitland takes care to know that which was known to Glanvill and Bracton; but he does not for that reason neglect Brunner or Gierke, Esmein or Viollet. A piece of continental evidence suggested by the history of the Inquisition points to the reason why in England alone the public trial of primitive Teutonic civilisation survived through the Middle Ages. It survived because the Inquisition was never introduced into this country, and England had no Inquisition because at the critical period it was singularly unfertile in heresy.

"It has generally been apprehended," writes Reeves in the Preface to the First Edition of the *History of English Law* (1783), "that much light might be thrown on our statutes by the civil history of the times in which they were made; but it will be found on enquiry that these expectations are rarely satisfied." It would be difficult to find in a single sentence a more complete measure of the gulf which separates Pollock and Maitland's *History of English Law* from the book which it supplanted. Reeves wrote in an unhistorical age and with imperfect materials. "Let us think," wrote Maitland, "what Reeves had at his disposal, what we have at our disposal. He had the Statute Book, the Year Books in a bad and clumsy edition, the old text-books in bad and clumsy editions. He made no use of Domesday Book; he had not the *Placitorum Abbreviatio*, nor Palgrave's *Rotuli Curiæ Regis*; he had no Parliament rolls, Pipe, Patent, Close, Fine, Hundred Rolls, no proceedings of the King's Council, no early Chancery proceedings, not a cartulary, not a manorial extent nor a manorial roll; he had not Nichol's *Britton*, nor Pike's nor Harwood's *Year Books*, nor Stubbs' *Select Charters*, nor Bigelow's *Placita Anglo-Normannica*; he had no collection of Anglo-Saxon land-books, only a very faulty collection of Anglo-Saxon dooms, while the early history of law in Normandy was utter darkness." And in addition to this he did not believe that the general history of a people could throw illumination upon its law. It is a sufficient commentary upon such a view to read Maitland's opening paragraph upon the Norman Conquest.

The state of English law in the twelfth century cannot be explained unless we look beyond the strict legal sphere. Explanations which seemed adequate even to the great Stubbs—the action of race upon race, the fusion of law with law, the analogy of a river formed by two streams, of a chemical compound formed of two elements—do not satisfy Maitland. The process was far more complex. It was affected by influences which had nothing whatever to do with the law of Normandy or with the law of England before the Conquest, by the rebellion of the Norman feudatories, by the characters of certain great men, by the strong political centralization, even by so accidental a fact as that the Conqueror had three sons instead of one. Economic, political, personal forces must all be reckoned up in the account.

While the pages of the *History* were passing through the press, two other works had been planned and were already partially accomplished. In his edition of the *Note Book* Maitland had proclaimed the necessity for a new edition of Bracton, an edition based not upon inferior manuscripts but upon the best manuscripts, and accompanied by an adequate critical apparatus. Such a task would demand many years of painful toil and Maitland had more pressing calls upon his energies. Nevertheless he regarded it as important to arrive at a definite conclusion with regard to one fundamental question respecting his favourite author. What was the precise extent and character of Bracton's indebtedness to Roman Law? Sir Henry Maine in his famous lectures upon *Ancient Law*, published in 1860, went so far as to assert that Bracton "put off on his countrymen as a compendium of pure English law a treatise of which the entire form and two thirds of the contents was directly borrowed from the *Corpus Juris.*" But the amount of matter which Bracton directly borrowed from the *Corpus Juris* was comparatively insignificant, "not a thirteenth part of the book"; the Devonshire justice went for his Roman law not to the original springs but to a famous Italian doctor. Dr Carl Guterbock established the fact that large portions of Bracton's *De Legibus* were derived from the works of Azo, a Bolognese Jurist who flourished at the end of the twelfth and at the beginning of the thirteenth century, and whose fame endured throughout the Middle Ages. But what was the precise measure of Bracton's obligation to "the master of all the masters of the laws"? It was Maitland's opinion that the debt might easily be overstated. In order that the matter might be thoroughly cleared up he planned a volume for the Selden Society which should exhibit in parallel columns the text of the Bolognese *Summa* and the corresponding portions of Bracton. From this he drew three conclusions, that Bracton's obligations to Roman Jurisprudence were small in extent, that Bracton was an indifferent Romanist, and thirdly that Bracton only borrowed from Roman law when he had no English cases to cite. Bracton was, in fact, a thorough Englishman. Like everyone else in the Middle Ages he regarded Roman law as a source of authority to which recourse should be had when the stock of home-bred law ran out, but it was improbable that he had ever received a University training in the *Leges* and it is certain that he was far more comfortable with his English writs and his English plea-rolls than with the elegant refinements of the Code or the Digest.

" Bracton and Azo" did more than define the " Romanesque" quality of the great treatise ; it was a brilliant contribution to the scholarly edition of the future. The best manuscript (*Bodl. Digby* 222) was minutely described, four others carefully collated, and fifteen in all examined. One of the features of the Digby manuscript, which, though not a perfect copy of the autograph, appeared to Maitland on many grounds to be the best approach to the autograph to which research had attained, was the presence of a large mass of additional matter written in the margins. Now these marginalia were not glosses but additions to the text and additions possessing a peculiar value from the fact that they came from Bracton himself. " If the annotator was not Bracton he had just Bracton's interests and just Bracton's style." In later manuscripts some or all of this supplementary matter is received into the text but "too often at inappropriate places." Accordingly the future editor of the Treatise will be obliged to pay special heed to these "addiciones"; and, to smooth a path which will be none too easy, Maitland made a list of more than a hundred and fifty passages in the printed text of 1869 which in the Digby manuscript stand in the margin. Such labour occupying but a few pages of Appendix looks but a small thing on paper, and is too technical to interest the general reader : but scholars will measure the devotion which it implies; and the future edition of the *De Legibus* will be based on the results of Maitland's unsparing toil among the Bracton manuscripts in London and Oxford, Cheltenham and Eton.

VII.

In the summer vacation of 1895 Maitland wrote as follows to his friend, Mr R. L. Poole, the editor of the *English Historical Review* :

" I have been thinking of asking you to let me have a talk about Domesday. I have a great deal of stuff written. Some of it Round has forestalled, as I knew he would. At one time it was to have gone into the book that Pollock and I published. Then I did not wish to collide with Round and now I know that Vinogradoff is again at work, and there are many economic and social questions which I would rather leave to him. So I have not and shall not have enough that is new to make a book. On the other hand I have a few legal theories that I should like to put before the public in one form or another. What do you think ? Would the *E. H. R.* bear a little Domesday—two or three articles ? However I will stand out of Frederick Pollock's way if he has anything to say, so when you have ascertained his intentions will you tell me whether you would take some papers from me. I would begin with some talk about Round's work of which I think very highly. I hope that you will say first what you think; in no case shall I be disappointed."

The publication of the *Domesday Inquest* was begun in 1783 and completed in 1816 and in the whole range of English history there is no authority alike so crucial in importance and so difficult of interpretation. Of the value of this unique statistical record compiled from the returns of local jurors twenty years after the Norman Conquest there has never been any dispute. Long before the text was published it was the subject of antiquarian monographs and the established base of local histories and genealogical enquiries. Transcripts of parts of Domesday were scattered up and down the country in public and private collections, and its fame was spread by the testimony of John Selden, who pronounced that, so far as he knew, it was by several centuries the oldest official record extant in autograph in the whole Christian world. The enterprise of the Record Commission made the record accessible to the student, and a popular Introduction to Domesday, written by Sir Henry Ellis in 1833, provided a pleasant quarry for the general historian whose soul was not vexed by the fundamental problems of Anglo-Norman society and finance.

But the survey was not understood. Even Freeman, who devoted to it a whole chapter in the fifth volume of the *Norman Conquest*, did not attack the central difficulties. He was a political historian, and appreciated the political interest of the record; but this is not the main interest. The survey owes its chief importance to the fact that it exhibits the social, economic and legal condition of the English people twenty years after the shock of the Norman Conquest.

Light gradually broke in from the labours of the specialist, from Eyton and Hamilton and above all from Mr Horace Round, who, in two brilliant papers composed for the Domesday Commemoration of 1888, cleared up some of the crucial questions connected with Domesday measures and Domesday finance. But perhaps the most exciting contribution proceeded from a book which was neither the work of a professed specialist nor yet a Domesday monograph. Mr Seebohm's *English Village Community* appeared in 1876 and gave English readers for the first time a luminous account of that system of medieval husbandry which the enclosures of the eighteenth century did not entirely avail to obliterate[1]. Alike in its methods and conclusions the *English Village Community* was an epoch-making book. Reversing the ordinary chronological procedure and arguing from comparatively recent periods, where evidence is abundant, past the cartularies and extents of the twelfth and thirteenth centuries, past Domesday to the twilight of the Saxon land-books and the darker regions beyond, Mr Seebohm arrived at the conclusion that the English village community was the outgrowth of the Roman vill and that whatever might have been the case in other regions of national life there was no breach in the continuity of agrarian history. A bold

---

[1] The leading characteristics of the system had been pointed out as early as 1821 by the Danish scholar, O. C. Olufsen, and received much further illustration from the labours of Georg Hanssen of Göttingen, whose papers [collected in 1880–4 under the title *Agrarhistorische Abhandlungen*] date back to 1835.

challenge was flung against the tradition accepted by a line of distinguished scholars from Kemble and Von Maurer to Freeman and Stubbs. The English village community was the offspring, not of a community of Teuton freemen, but of a system moulded by the Latin genius and rooted in slavery. The influence of Roman Britain was not so insignificant after all, nor was the completeness of the Teutonic Conquest so complete. In the most fundamental part of her economic and social texture England was indebted not to Germany but to Rome. The battle between the Germanists and the Romanists brought into clearer relief the importance of Domesday studies. Questions of Domesday nomenclature—the meaning for instance of the Domesday hide—acquired a new relevance, and might turn the scale in grave issues. A large hide of a hundred and twenty acres would naturally imply an early society of free peasant proprietors, a small hide of thirty acres might, on the contrary, be fitted into the Romanist hypothesis. Domesday was the key to the position. Properly interpreted, it would not only explain the influence of the Conquest, but throw light upon the Anglo-Saxon land-system and the obscure problem of agrarian origins. Mr Round's further contributions to the understanding of the Record, which were published in *Feudal England* in 1895, were recognised as having a bearing upon the largest problems of English history.

It was left to Sir Frederick Pollock to appraise Mr Round's work in the pages of the *English Historical Review*. Maitland's researches, which were pushed to a conclusion with astonishing rapidity, appeared in 1896

in a volume entitled *Domesday Book and Beyond—
Three Essays in the Early History of England.*
The first essay was called " Domesday Book," the
second " England before the Conquest," the third
" The Hide." The title was chosen to indicate
the fact that Maitland had followed the retrogres-
sive method from the known to the unknown which
Mr Seebohm had pursued with such admirable effect.
" Domesday Book appears to me not as the known
but as the knowable.   The Beyond is still very dark :
but the way to it lies through the Norman record.   The
result is given to us ; the problem is to find cause and
process."

Identity of method, however, did not imply identical
conclusions.   Eight years before Maitland had revised
the sheets of a remarkable study of *Villainage in
England*, by Paul Vinogradoff, the conclusions of which
were decidedly adverse to the Romanist hypothesis of
servile origins ; but whereas Vinogradoff had confined
himself to the analysis of agrarian conditions as revealed
by the post-Domesday evidence, Maitland made his
assault upon the mysterious fortress of the great
survey itself.   " That in some sort I have been
endeavouring to answer Mr Seebohm, I cannot conceal
from myself or from others.   A hearty admiration of
his *English Village Community* is one main source
of this book.   That the task of disputing his conclusions
might have fallen to stronger hands than mine I well
know.   I had hoped that by this time Professor Vinogradoff's *Villainage in England* would have had a
sequel.   When that sequel comes (and may it come
soon) my provisional answer can be forgotten."

All scientific work is in a sense provisional, and *Domesday Book and Beyond* contains some theories which we believe that Maitland would have subsequently revised. But whether it be regarded as a model of acute and substantial investigation, or weighed by the mass of its contributions to the permanent fabric of historical understanding and knowledge, it will assuredly rank among the classical monographs of historical science. Maitland did not profess to cover the whole field of economic and social development. He approached the history of the eleventh century mainly as a lawyer anxious to analyse the legal conceptions of that age, and fully conscious of the extreme difficulty and delicacy of his task. " The grown man," he remarks, " will find it easier to think the thoughts of the schoolboy than to think the thoughts of the baby. And yet the doctrine that our remote forefathers being simple folk had simple law dies hard. Too often we allow ourselves to suppose that, could we but get back to the beginning, we should find that all was intelligible and should then be able to watch the process whereby simple ideas were smothered under subtleties and technicalities. But it is not so. Simplicity is the outcome of technical subtlety; it is the goal not the starting-point. As we go backwards the familiar outlines become blurred; the ideas become fluid, and instead of the simple we find the indefinite.... We must not be in a hurry to get to the beginning of the long history of law. Very slowly we are making our way towards it. The history of law must be a history of ideas. It must represent not merely what people have done and said, but what men have thought in bygone ages. The task of reconstructing ancient ideas is hazardous and can only be accomplished little by little. In particular there lies a besetting danger for us in the barbarian's use of a language which is too good for his thought. Mistakes then are easy, and when committed they will be fatal and fundamental mistakes. If for example we introduce the *persona ficta* too soon, we shall be doing worse than if we armed Hengest and Horsa with machine guns or pictured the Venerable Bede correcting proofs for the press; we shall have built upon a crumbling foundation." The main argument of the book was directed against the view that the English manorial system was the outcome of the Roman villa. The English language, the names of our English villages, were sufficient to rebut the hypothesis that the bulk of the agricultural population was of Celtic blood descended from the slaves or *coloni* of Roman times. Romanism would give no rational explanation of the state of things revealed by the Domesday survey in the northern and eastern counties. Nor would it explain seignorial justice. It was shown that at the time of the survey England was still incompletely manorialised, that the Domesday manors varied indefinitely in size and type, that some had freeholders, some not, that in some there were courts, in others none, and that no general proposition respecting either jurisdictional rights or agrarian continuity would apply to them universally. That the manors of Domesday were mainly tilled by villeins who in a certain sense were unfree, was doubtless true, but there was evidence to show that the position of the agricultural class had deteriorated during the period which elapsed between the Conquest and the survey, and many calamities natural or fiscal, a murrain, a hailstorm, a levy of Danegeld, a judicial fine, might be enumerated to account for a gradual decline in the status of the rural population during the Saxon age.

Evidence from an entirely different quarter supported the main conclusion. Far back at the beginning of the eighth century Bede had spoken of the hide as the normal holding of the English householder. By a train of very subtle and elaborate calculations Maitland came to the conclusion that the hide of which Bede spoke and to which Domesday testifies contained 120 arable acres,—a tenement too large for any serf or semi-servile *colonus* and therefore precluding the idea that the manorial system was dominant in England in very early Saxon times. How then did the system arise? Maitland advanced an ingenious hypothesis, admitting, " that nothing which could be called a strict proof could be offered "—that the word *manerium* as used by the Domesday commissioners possessed a technical sense. Domesday was a fiscal inquest; the object of the commissioners was the collection of geld; geld is collected from persons who live in houses and the word *manerium* means a house. For the fiscal purpose of these Norman officials *manerium* meant " the house at which geld is charged." The lord, in other words, was made responsible to the state for the payment of geld from his demesne land and the land of his villeins, and was bound to take measures to see that the tax was paid by such freemen and socmen as might be attached to his manor. The theory was not of course intended to provide a solution for the main problem. It suggested an answer to the question "What is the technical meaning attached to the word *manerium* in Domesday?" it revealed one of the possible forces which may have contributed to manorial dependence: but it did not explain or pretend to explain either the forces which made for the subjection of the peasantry to seignorial justice or the peculiar system of ownership and cultivation which was distinctive of the manor.

The problem was no doubt mainly economic, but it possessed its legal aspect. A brilliant analysis of Anglo-Saxon *diplomata*, which could hardly have been accomplished save by a practised lawyer, revealed the fact that the Anglo-Saxon kings had been freely alienating public powers, fiscal and jurisdictional, to churches and private persons. The Saxon land-book does not transfer land, but superiorities over land. It may be true that the gift has all the appearance of being unconditional, "granted as a reward for past services, not as a condition for the performance of future services"; but the contrast between the deeds of the Saxon and Norman period is one rather of form than of substance. Every Saxon grant of "immunities" reserves the "trinoda necessitas," that fundamental military obligation which lay upon every freeman, and if that service was not performed the land was forfeit to the king. Then again land-loans were not uncommon, and land-loans and land-gifts shaded imperceptibly into one another. All the lineaments of the feudal land system are already visible in the later Anglo-Saxon period. The feudal formula of dependent

tenure is known; the exercise of jurisdictional rights
by private persons is a familiar fact; in places one
could even see, "a four-storied feudal edifice." No
large historical transformation is matter for unqualified
regret. Feudalism was a necessary stage in the education and development of the barbarian world. "There
are indeed historians who have not yet abandoned the
habit of speaking of feudalism as though it were a
disease of the body politic. Now the word feudalism
is and always will be an inexact term, and, no doubt, at
various times and places there emerge phenomena
which may with great propriety be called feudal, and
which come of evil and make for evil. But if we use
the term, and often we do, in a very wide sense, then
feudalism will appear to us as a natural and even a
necessary stage in our history. If we use the term in
this wide sense, then (the barbarian conquests being
given to us as an unalterable fact) feudalism means
civilisation, the separation of employment, a division
of labour, the possibility of national defence, the possibility of art, science, literature and learned leisure ; the
cathedral, the scriptorium, the library are as truly the
work of feudalism as is the baronial castle."

One of the inevitable consequences of the process
was a confusion in legal ideas. Distinctions which in
the classical Roman law were clearly drawn became
obliterated in the Middle Ages. Ownership and
sovereignty, rents and taxes, public and private rights,
became blended together in one large, hazy, undistinguished concept. Even the contrast between freedom
and unfreedom which appears to the modern mind so
elementary and so logical did not fit the intricate

economic facts of the eleventh century. Of freedom there were many grades and many criteria. In one sense the villein was free, in another sense unfree, as a combination of forces fiscal, economic, penal were assimilating the rural population free and servile to the hybrid type. "Freedom is measured along several different scales. At one time it is to the power of alienation or withdrawal that attention is attracted, at another to the number and kind of services and 'customs' that the man must render to his lord." The closer the facts of Domesday were scrutinised the more impossible did it appear to arrive at exact definitions.

Maitland's subtle powers of analysis were never shown to better advantage than in this attempt to rethink "the common thoughts of our forefathers, their common thoughts about common things." We doubt whether any historian had ever set himself down so seriously to get inside the medieval mind. The pompous phraseology in the early *diplomata* does not deceive him, for he knows that the romanesque terms neither express the thoughts nor represent the facts of a barbarian age. Large phrases confidently used by modern historians, such as "property" or "joint liability," must be closely scrutinised before they can be applied to a remote age; property is a bundle of rights, and with every advance in economic progress, in material aspirations, in intellectual definition, rights and powers multiply, the conception of *dominium* becomes more intensive, fuller of content and discriminations. There is no fixed immutable limit to the implications of such a concept. The Saxon chieftain learnt the extent of his powers in the process of

alienating them to the Church, as some African chieftain tempted by gin and rifles may acquire a knowledge
that land is not made for sheep alone, but may also
yield gold and diamonds. But as the barbarian is
vague, so also he is for all his materialism an idealist.
" He sees things not as they are but as they might
conveniently be. Every householder has a hide;
every hide has 120 acres of arable; every hide is worth
one pound a year; every householder has a team;
every team is of eight oxen; every team is worth one
pound. If all this be not so, then it ought to be so,
and must be deemed to be so. Then by a Procrustean
system he packs the complex and irregular facts into
his scheme!" It is no light enterprise to understand
the puzzled and inadequate thought which lies at the
basis of our social history; Maitland believed that the
reward was worthy of the effort.

It appeared to Maitland that one of the obstacles
to an exact understanding of the past was the general
acceptance of the idea that a normal programme could
be laid down for the human race. Even if there were
sufficient evidence to show that each independent
portion of the human race must move through a fated
series of changes, it remained a fact that the rapidly
progressive groups had not been independent. " Our
Anglo-Saxon ancestors did not arrive at the alphabet
or at the Nicene Creed by traversing a long series of
'stages'; they leapt to the one and to the other." And
again the complexity and interdependence of human
affairs render it impossible to hope for scientific laws
which will formulate a sequence of stages in any one
province of men's activity. Consequently it was un-

wise to fill up the blanks that occurred in the history
of one nation by institutions and processes which had
been observed in another quarter. Even if it were
proved that the Roman *gens* was a close agnatic group,
and that the house community was the primitive unit
of Roman society, we should not "force our reluctant
forefathers through agnatic *gentes* and house communities." In particular we were not entitled to assume
without further enquiry that the early English village
community owned land.

Such criticisms, implying as they did that the
Roman evidence had been accredited with a wider
relevance than it did or could possess, were calculated
to abate the more sanguine claims alike of comparative
jurisprudence and of anthropology. In a subsequent
paper contributed to the Eranus Club Maitland re-
curred to his central thesis, that the experience of the
progressive nations was interdependent and unique,
and incapable, for that very reason, of affording a basis
for an inductive science of politics. It is among the
many refreshing qualities of Maitland's work that while
he is always close to his facts he is never out of the
atmosphere of large and animating ideas.

In the matter of early English land-holding
Maitland put the individualist case with great cogency.
While admitting co-operation he did not find decisive
evidence of common ownership either in town or
country. The village community was not a body that
could declare the law of the tribe or nation. It had
no court, no jurisdiction. If moots were held in it,
these would be comparable rather to meetings of
shareholders than to sessions of a tribunal. In short,

the village landowners formed a group of men whose economic affairs were inextricably intermixed; but this was almost the only principle that made them a unit, unless and until the state began to use the township as its organ for the maintenance of the peace and the collection of the taxes. That is the reason why we read little of the township in our Anglo-Saxon dooms. Even in the German community there was a solid core of individualism! It is possible that Maitland over-rated the "automatic" character of early agrarian life; that he argued too much from the silence of the dooms, that his principal tests were too predominantly legal; and that more may be said for the older theory than he was able at that time to discover in *Domesday Book and Beyond.* But the considerations which he submitted were substantial considerations, and in any picture which is drawn of the early state of landholding in this country room will have to be made for a measure of individualism, if not equal to that which Maitland claimed, greater at least than the earlier theory had admitted.

VIII.

In the course of his researches for the *History of English Law* Maitland had been drawn into the unfamiliar region of ecclesiastical jurisprudence, a department of knowledge once of the highest importance throughout Europe, but, save for one exception, fallen into complete desuetude at the English Universities ever since the study of the Canon Law was proscribed by Henry VIII. The exception was provided by William Stubbs. That great master of medieval history had from his Oxford Chair delivered and subsequently published two lectures upon the Canon Law in England. A stout patriot and a high Anglican, Stubbs was concerned to exhibit the continuity of the English Church before and after the Reformation ; and both in his Oxford lectures and in a famous report drawn up for the Royal Commission on Ecclesiastical Courts he gave the weight of his authority to the opinion that the Canon Law of Rome, though held to be of great authority in England during the Middle Ages, was not recognised to be binding on the Courts Christian of this country. The verdict of so fine a scholar was eagerly welcomed by men of High Church opinions. If the Canon Law was not binding, then the Church of England was never in the full sense ultramontane, and the changes of the sixteenth century did not amount to revolution. Zealots went further still. There were those who, as Maitland wittily observed, seemed to believe that the Church of England was " Protestant before the Reformation and Catholic afterwards."

In the quarrel between the Highs and Lows Maitland had no interest. Then, as always, he was a dissenter from all the Churches : but historical truth was precious to him, and in the course of the summer of 1895, while engaged in the preparation of a course of lectures upon the Canon Law, he became gradually aware that the received opinion could no longer stand. The agent of his conversion, if conversion it can be called, was the *Provinciale* of William Lyndwood, a popular text-book written in 1430 by the principal official of the Archbishop of Canterbury, and representative of the accepted opinion in the century preceding the Protestant Reformation. The following letter to Mr R. L. Poole explains the genesis of a book which has permanently deflected the current of historical opinion.

HORSEPOOLS,
STROUD.
15*th August*, 1895.

I ought to have been writing lectures about the history of the Canon Law. Instead of so doing I have been led away into a lengthy discourse on Lyndwood. I have come to a result that seems to be heterodox, but I do not know exactly how heterodox it is and should be extremely grateful if you would give me your opinion upon a question which lies rather within your studies than within mine. It seems to me clear, that in Lyndwood's view the law laid down in the three great papal law-books is statute law for the English ecclesiastical courts and overrules all the provincial constitutions, and further that apart from the law contained in these books the Church of England has hardly any law—in short there is next to nothing that can be called *English* Canon Law. I must wait until I am again in Cambridge to read what has been written about this matter in modern times, but any word of counsel that you can give me will be treasured. From a remark that you once made I inferred that in your opinion our Church

historians have been too patriotic. I feel pretty sure
of this after spending two months with Lyndwood,
and if I find that my conclusions about the law of our
ecclesiastical courts are at variance with the prevail-
ing doctrine, may be I shall print what I have been
writing, that is to say if either *L. Q. R.* or *E. H. R.*,
will let me trail my coat through its pages.

Roman Canon Law in the Church of England
appeared in 1898. It was a collection of six essays,
one of which—the delightful story of the Deacon who
turned Jew for the love of a Jewess—had been published as far back as 1886. Of the rest the decisive
part consisted of articles contributed to the *English
Historical Review* in 1896 and 1897. So far as a
case can be demolished by argument, the case for
the legal continuity of the Church in England was
demolished by Maitland. He proved that the Popes'
decretals were regarded as absolutely binding by our
English canonists; that throughout Christendom the
Pope was regarded as the Universal Ordinary or
supreme source of Jurisdiction; that a considerable
portion of the Canon Law was built out of English
cases; that the provincial constitutions in England
were of the nature of bye-laws and insignificant, while
the libraries of our canonists were filled with foreign
treatises; in fine, that the thirty-two Commissioners
who set their names to the opinion that the ecclesiastical judges in England were not bound by the
statutes which the Popes had decreed for all the
faithful would have been condemned by any English
ecclesiastical tribunal in the Middle Ages as guilty of

heresy. No doubt portions of the Canon Law were not as a matter of fact enforced in England, but this was not because the Courts Christian rejected them, but because the Temporal power would not permit their enforcement.

Royal prohibitions did not prove the existence of a national Canon Law. "To prove that we must see an ecclesiastical judge, whose hands are free and who has no 'prohibition' to fear, rejecting a decretal because it infringes the law of the English Church or because that Church has not received it." Whatever might be the view of a late age, no such testimony was forthcoming before the breach with Rome. Indeed the "one great work of our English canonist in the fifteenth century" showed that the position which had been attributed to the English Church in the Middle Ages was alien to its whole way of thought. In the age of the conciliar movement, when men of liberal temperament were urging that the Pope was subject to a general council, William Lyndwood evidenced nothing but "a conservative curialism."

The book was necessarily controversial, but written with that complete absence of the polemical spirit which characterised all Maitland's work. "I hope and trust," he wrote to Mr Poole, September 12, 1898, "that you were not very serious when you said that the bishop was sore. I feel for him a respect so deep, that if you told me that the republication of my essays would make him more unhappy than a sane man is whenever people dissent from him, I should be in great doubt what to do. It is not too late to destroy all or some of the sheets. I hate to bark at the heels of a great man whom I admire, but tried hard to seem as well as to be respectful."

An accident of friendship drew Maitland still further into the tormented sea of controversial church history. Lord Acton was appointed Regius Professor of Modern History at Cambridge in 1895, and, despite radical differences of creed and outlook, soon discovered in Maitland a spirit as ardent and disinterested as his own. Outwardly there was a great contrast between the two men, Maitland frail and delicate, his pale eager face a lamp of humour and curiosity, Acton massive, reserved, deliberate; but they understood one another, and soon came to share a common interest in a great literary enterprise. One day Acton propounded to Maitland the scheme for a great Cambridge history written upon the combined plan which was already familiar in France and Germany. It was to be a Universal History, a history of the whole world from the first beginnings to the present day, written by an army of specialists, and concentrating the latest results of special study. Maitland suggested that a more modest plan, a history of modern Europe since the Reformation, would prove to be more practical, and in this view Acton concurred.

The *Cambridge Modern History* covered a period which did not properly fall within Maitland's special range of study; but he was taken into counsel as to the general execution of the plan, and persuaded to contribute a chapter upon the Anglican Settlement and the Scottish Reformation. That Acton should have chosen Maitland for this particular piece of work may cause some surprise. The ground was intricate,

sown with pitfalls and clouded with controversy, and
Maitland had made no special study of the sixteenth
century upon the political or religious side.   On the
other hand he could bring to the task a cool, dis-
passionate judgment, a fine power for appraising
historical evidence, and a singular and exact felicity
in the expression of delicate shades of certainty and
doubt.   That he stood outside the Churches might
have been a disqualification, had devotional impulses
been the staple consideration in the question, or if the
banners of rival confessions were not already waving
on the battle field; but the age of Elizabeth was
theological rather than religious, and it was of the first
importance to obtain the verdict of a thoroughly im-
partial mind upon a subject which could never be
treated by a churchman without some suspicion
of partisanship attaching to his results.   Maitland
accepted the task with misgivings, and discharged it
with characteristic thoroughness.   In an astonishingly
short space of time his mind filled itself up with the
reports of French and Spanish ambassadors, with the
theological treatises and the political intrigues of sixteenth century Europe.   A month or so after he had
taken the plunge he was talking of Caraffa and Cecil
as if he had known them all his life, and seemed to
have gathered up the whole complicated web of
European policy into his hands.   He did not content
himself with mastering and reproducing the voluminous
literature of the subject; some pretty little discoveries,
some "Elizabethan gleanings" were contributed to
the *English Historical Review*, and gave evidence of
refined investigations which did not stop at printed

material. Results which might have furnished the
theme for a substantial volume were packed into a
chapter of forty pages. Critics complained of obscurity
not of thought but of allusion; others, imperfectly
versed in Tudor history, of a defective sympathy
with religious emotion. The first charge is true ; for
Maitland was undoubtedly over-allusive, not from
ostentation but from absorption and from a tendency
common to learned and modest men to credit the
general reader with more knowledge than he is likely
to possess. To the second allegation it is some reply
that Maitland was inclined to attribute the most
decisive act in the period, Elizabeth's resolve to reject
the Roman overtures, to religious rather than to
political motives.

With habitual modesty Maitland disclaimed the
possession of the gift of narration. He would say
that he could not tell a story ; and the character of
his historical work was not adapted to exercise the
story-telling gift. But if his narrative has not the
liquid flow of some accredited masters of the art,
it is entirely devoid of some common defects. It is
never indefinite, flabby or verbose, on the contrary it
is full of pith and fire, proceeding by a series of brief
vivid touches which take root in the memory and ripen
there. It would be easy to select from the chapter
upon the Scottish Reformation and the Anglican
settlement a *florilegium* of passages which, for keen-
ness of insight and terseness of expression, could not
easily be surpassed. It is a style which gives the
impression not only of clairvoyance and watchfulness
as to small details, transient motives and ephemeral

phases of opinion, but also of a sense of the fundamental significance of things and of their relevance in
the general march of progress. Every stroke is made
to tell. In general nothing is so tedious as a history
constructed upon severe philosophical principles. The
argument swallows up the life ; the characters become
faint and evanescent ; the colour put upon one event
is shaded by the reflection of events which follow, and
an oft repeated major premise leads through an appropriate selection of devitalised incidents to a familiar
conclusion. Maitland's fragment of Reformation history is philosophical in the best sense. It is alive to
the ultimate principles of belief and conduct which
governed men and women in the years when the
Thirty-Nine Articles were in the making; but it is
also very vivid and concrete. The tale has been told
more fully, more comfortably, with a greater display of
picturesque circumstance, but never with more intellect,
or with so exact an appreciation of the chronological
order in which successive phases of belief and opinion
revealed themselves. Instead of history ready-made
Maitland gave us history in the making, antedating
nothing and excluding with a care no less scrupulous
than Gardiner's the world's knowledge of to-morrow
from the world's knowledge of to-day. More than
one fairy story dissolved at his touch, among others
the tale of a Convocation summoned in 1559 to
consent to the Act of Uniformity. The parent of the
legend, an Anglican Canon, with a comical misappre-
hension of his antagonist's resources, ventured to
measure swords with Maitland who had exposed his
shortcomings in a Magazine. The encounter was

amusing and decisive. It was also characteristic of some English peculiarities. We are a nation of bold amateurs. A German pastor who had been corrected by Savigny upon some points of history would hardly have returned to the charge without betraying some suspicion that his enterprise was unpromising if not forlorn.

IX.

Not the least brilliant passage in *Domesday Book and Beyond* was a novel theory as to the origin and early history of the English Borough. The question of municipal origins had produced a library of controversial literature upon the Continent. One writer developed the town from the feudal domain, another from the "immunity," a third from the guild, a fourth from the market, a fifth from the free village, and there were combinations and permutations of these and other factors. Maitland was impressed by the arguments of Dr Keutgen of Jena, who found the origin and criterion of the German borough in its fortification. The idea transplanted into Maitland's mind became surprisingly fruitful. Scattered fragments of evidence seemed to confirm the surmise that in the English Midlands at least the county town was the county fortress, owing its origin to military necessity and supported by a variety of artificial arrangements. There was the evidence of language, for borough originally means a fortified house; the evidence of the map, for in many counties of England the county town is somewhere near the centre; the evidence of warlike stress, for the Danes were foemen even more terrible than those wild Hungarians against whom Henry the Fowler built his Saxon "burhs"; the evidence of Domesday Book, showing contrivances at once careful and varied for maintaining town walls and town garrisons; and here and there a gleam of light from older documents, from the Burghal Hidage of the tenth century, or from a charter of King Alfred. The argument, which was expounded with beautiful clearness and ingenuity, led on to the conclusion that the town court was the product of "tenural hetero-geneity," for the garrison men holding of different lords would need a special court to decide their con-troversies. There was thus a greater degree of governmental artifice in the process than had hitherto been suspected. The borough was not merely a very prosperous village; it was a unit in a scheme of national defence; a fortified town maintained by a district for military purposes with "mural houses" and "knight guilds" and a miscellaneous garrison contributed by shire thegns. By degrees trade, com-merce, agriculture, the interests of the market and the town fields would overpower the military characteristics of the county stronghold. But the scheme should not be pressed too far; "no general theory will tell the story of every or any particular town."

In the autumn of 1897 Maitland gave the Ford Lectures in Oxford. The foundation was recent, and Maitland was chosen to succeed S. R. Gardiner, who had delivered the opening course in the previous year. Gardiner had lectured extempore on "Cromwell's Place in History"; Maitland delivered a series of carefully written dissertations upon "Township and Borough," a subject as little likely, one would think, to hold together an audience in the Schools as any that could be imagined. The ordinary man is not interested in law, still less in medieval law, and less again in the metaphysics of medieval law; but a large and constant audience was interested in Maitland. His style of lecturing was distinctive and original—the voice deep, grave, expressive, the delivery dramatic, the substance compounded of subtle speculation and playful wit and recondite learning. The lectures which were learnt by heart were delivered with a verve and earnestness which impressed many a hearer who was entirely indifferent to the particular issues or to the whole region of learning to which they belonged. When and how did the Borough become a Corporation? Who owned the Town fields? In what sense was the medieval borough a land-owning community? What did King John mean when he granted the vill of Cambridge to the burgesses and their heirs? With Maitland's artful spells upon her Oxford felt that such questions as these might be very grave and not a little gay.

X.

The wonderful work which has here been imperfectly described was accomplished under a shadow. Maitland, who was never really a strong man, was, even before his marriage, not without warnings that he was overtaxing his physical resources. When he delivered his inaugural lecture he was already conscious that his days might be few. " I see again," writes one who was present, "the dim room, the grey light and the shadowy but inspired fragileness of the lecturer who was then fighting a very serious illness.... It was no ordinary lecture, rather a sort of sermon, grave and beautiful with its solemn call to work, even though that work might lie in humble and obscure fields. And the impression that was perhaps most immediately insistent, seeming to underlie each word and sentence, was that the speaker felt the hours of his own work to be already numbered and but few." In 1889, the year after his election to the Downing Chair, a doctor pronounced over him a sentence from which there is generally no successful appeal. " I very much want to see you again " he wrote to a friend, March 12, 1889, "and I don't know that I can wait for another year; this I say rather seriously and *only to you*; many things are telling me that I have not got unlimited time at my command and I have to take things very easily."

Devoted nursing, great care in diet, and a resolute avoidance of many of the pleasant things of life enabled the work to proceed as buoyantly as ever. There were bouts of illness and pain, when the French novelist and especially the beloved and well-known Balzac had to be invoked, but there were also periods of revival and at one time an assurance that the alarming symptoms had disappeared. But in truth the malady was never dislodged. "Slowly it is doing for me; but quite slowly," he wrote to a friend in 1899, "and it may cheer you to know that I have had ten happy and busy years under the ban." In the summer and autumn of that tenth year there was a sudden change for the worse and it became clear that Maitland could no longer winter in England. "If I have to sing a Nunc Dimittis," he wrote to Mr R. L. Poole, "it will run 'Quia oculi mei viderunt originalem Actum de Uniformitate primi anni Reg. Eliz.' Few can say as much....I think of a voyage to S. America as S. Africa looks too warm for a man of peace."

From 1898 the Maitlands were compelled to fly south with the approach of winter. Their regular resort was Grand Canary but once, in 1904, this was exchanged for Madeira. Like all other habits idleness requires cultivation and Maitland had never been idle. Under a tropical sky and with an exquisite sense of relief from physical pain he worked his writing muscles as busily as ever. In the first exile he translated that part of Otto Gierke's *Deutsche Genossenschaftrecht*, which dealt with medieval political theory, and published it with a brilliant Introduction. Later he copied manuscripts of the Year Books lent to him by the wise generosity of the Cambridge University Library and collated or transcribed photographs of those manuscripts which it was impossible to export. The last two winters were divided between the Year Books and the composition of a biography of Leslie Stephen, and so far was exile from being a holiday that the fruit of each winter spent in the fortunate islands was never less than the substantial part of the volume. Some letters shall speak of the impressions and activities of these years.

To Leslie Stephen.

HOTEL SANTA CATALINA,
LAS PALMAS,
GRAN CANARIA.

5 *Nov.* 1898.

I am beginning Guy Fawkes's day by sitting in the verandah before breakfast to write letters for a homeward-bound mail. Certainly it is enjoyable here and I mean to get good out of a delightful climate. Also I mean to convert your half promise of a visit into a whole, and without going beyond the truth I can say that there is a good deal here that should please you. At first sight I was repelled by the arid desolation of the island. I suppose that I ought to have been prepared for grasslessness, but somehow or another I was not. But then the wilderness is broken by patches of wonderful green—the green of banana fields. Wherever a little water can be induced to flow in artificial channels there are all manner of beautiful things to be seen. I have picked a date and mustered enough Spanish to buy me a pair of shoes in the "city" of Las Palmas—a dirty city it is with strange smells; but we are well outside of it. Between Las Palmas and its port there is a little English colony. This hotel is so English that they give me my bill in £ *s. d.* and my change in British hapence which have seen better days. Indeed now I know where our coppers go to when they have become too bad for use at home. Also the "library" of this hotel seems a sort of hades to which the bad three-voller is sent

after its decease.   But the proposition that all the
worst books collect there is (as you must be aware)
not convertible into the proposition that only bad
books come there, and I see a copy of a certain *Life
of Henry Fawcett* which you may have read.   I laze
away my time under verandahs and in gardens—but
am not wholly inactive.   Sometimes when it is cool I
walk some miles and explore country that is well worth
exploration.   By the time you come I shall be ready
for an ascent of our central range with you—it touches
6000 ft. I think, and by that time we shall be having
cooler weather.   Yesterday we were breathless: to-day
is cloudy but would be September in England.
    It is breakfast time and the porridge is good.

TO LESLIE STEPHEN.

Sᵗᵃ BRIGIDA,
MONTE,
G. CANARY.
9 *Jan.* 1899.

    I won't pretend but that I am disappointed by your
decision, the more so because my hopes of your advent
stood higher than Florence's and I had endeavoured to
argue that your half-promise was a valuable security.
However, I know that we are far from England, and
that you are unwilling to leave your household for any
long time.   Also the two last boats that have come
here suffered much in the Bay of Biscay and were
very late.   So I forgive, though I badly want someone
to walk with.   The time has come when I feel that

walks are pleasant and do me good, but that I am very tired of the contents of my own head. But even a solitary tramp is better than a day in bed, and I am really grateful to this magnificent climate and to those who sent me here. To those who cannot speak Spanish, and I cannot and never shall, the remoter parts of this island are not very accessible. I sometimes find myself beset by a troop of boys who take a fiendish pleasure in dogging the steps of an Englishman who obviously is deaf, dumb and mad. Attempts to reason with them only lead to shouts of Penny! or Tilling!—I cannot even persuade them that Tilling is not an English word. Still at times they leave me in peace and then I can be happy until the next crowd assembles.

To Leslie Stephen.

Hotel Sª Brigida,
Monte,
Grand Canary.
23 *Jan.* 1899.

I fear from your last letter that you may take too seriously what I said in play. No, there was no promise, only a certain hope that you might come here, and Reason (with a capital) tells me that your decision is wise and that you must not give up to Canarios what was meant for your home and the *Utilitarians.* I am really glad to think that you are booking them, and at times I envy you. However I cannot say that I am unhappy in my idleness. When I despaired of you for a companion, I took to myself the soundest looking man in a hotel full of invalids, and gat me up into the hills to accomplish the expedition that I had reserved for you, and we succeeded in mastering not indeed the highest, but the most prominent mountain of the island, if a mountain may be no more than 6000 feet high.   This raised me in my own conceit and certainly I had a very enjoyable time.   I doubt whether in any of your good ascents you can have seen so gorgeously coloured a view as that which I beheld.   A great part of the island lay below me; many of the rocks are bright orange and crimson and these are diversified by patches of brilliant green; the whole was framed in the blue of sky and sea.   It was like a raised map that had been over-coloured.

TO FREDERICK POLLOCK.

CASA PEÑATE,
MONTE.
Dec. 4, 1899.

Dated in Timelessness, but with you it may be some such day as Dec. 4, and I fancy that cent. XIX may still be persisting.   Dated also nominally at Hotel Quiney in Las Palmas where I preserve address for service, but de facto in the garden of a messuage or finca called or known by the name of Bateria in the pueblo of Sta Brigida—a fortlike structure which I hold as a monthly tenant—windows on four sides all with fine views—on ground floor lives major domo,

a hard-worked peasant savouring of the soil—first and
only other floor inhabited by me and mine, including
our one servant, a Germano-Swiss treasure acquired
as we left England—furniture a minimum and no
more would be useful—small boy coatless comes to
clean boots, run errands and the like, Pepé to wit—
much bargaining at house door with women who bring
victuals round and would rather have a chat than
money. Madame's mastery of their jargon surprises
me daily—I can rarely catch a word. One might fall
into vegetarianism here, such is the choice of vegetals.

Lies in the garden on a long chair mostly—has
there written for *Encyclop. Brit.* article on Hist. Eng.
Law—space assigned 8 only of their big pages:
consequently tight packing of centuries: work of a
bookless imagination—but dates were brought from
England. Qu. whether editor will suffer the few lines
given to J. Austin: they amount to j.a. $= 0°$. Now
turning to translate Gierke's chapt. on "Publicistic
Doctrine of M.A.[1]"—O.G. has given consent—will
make lectures (if I return) and possibly book—but
what to do with "Publicistic"? Am reading Creighton's
Papacy and Gardiner's *History*—may be well-informed
man some day. Harv. L. Rev. and King's Peace
came pleasantly—Alphabet not yet presented to babes
but reserved for approaching birthday when it will
delight. Meanwhile parents profit by it and are very
grateful.

Influence of climate on epistolary style—a certain

[1] Middle Ages. In 1900 Maitland published a translation of
part of Otto Gierke's (O.G.) *Das deutsche Genossenschaftrecht* under
the title *Political Theories of the Middle Ages.*

disjointedness. Can live here or rather can be content to vegetate. A tolerable course for the Lea Francis —some 5 miles long—lies not far away, but must shoulder her and climb a rocky path to reach it. No puncture yet. The alarums and the excursions of horrid war are but little heard here. Interesting talk last night at hotel with German Consul in Liberia much travelled in Africa—very unboerish but thinks we are in for a large affair—all good (says he) for (German) trade. Much that we buy here made in Germany,— they spread apace.

To Frederick Pollock.

Casa Peñate, Monte,
Las Palmas.

5 Jan. 1900.

I have been wasting too many of my hours in bed —and such hours too—and have consequently written few letters. Somehow or another I was chilled in the course of my voyage : I think it was on board the little Spanish steamer that brought me here from Teneriffe : and after a few days, during which I improvidently cycled to Las Palmas and found that I had to trudge back, I collapsed. However that episode I hope is over, and certainly we are in luck this year. For three weeks the weather has been magnificent ; no drop of rain has fallen and day after day the sun has shone. It is like the best English June and there is nothing that tells of midwinter except some leafless poplars and chestnuts. I brought out a minimum thermometer which has refused to register anything less than 54°.

I have been devouring too rapidly my small store of books since I have been cut off from the writing which I projected. What I have seen of my two MSS of the Year Books of Edward II tells me that there is a solid piece of work to be done. One of these MSS is much fuller than the printed book. I cannot understand what demand there can have been for that printed book: it is so very unintelligible—mere nonsense much of it.

The B.G.B. will have to wait—at least so I think at present—as I shall give all my working time to the Y.B.B.—but the volumes of *Materialien* are very interesting—especially so much as consists of the debates in the Reichstag[1]. By far the keenest debate was about damage done by hares and pheasants : the sportsmen of the Right were very keen about this matter.

...You will gather from this scrawl that I am recumbent in a garden—the fact is so and I won't deny it.

To Leslie Stephen.

22 *Jan.* 1900.

I can well believe that England is a gloomy place just now. Even here where I see few papers and few English folk, except the family, this ghastly affair sits

---

[1] The B.G.B. is the *Bürgerliche Gesetzbuch*. Maitland was reading Mugdan's *Die Gesammten Materialien zum Bürgerlichen Gesetzbuch*. The Y.B.B. are the Year-books.

heavily upon me and is always coming between me and my book: at the moment Gardiner's *History*: from which my thoughts flit off to England and the Transvaal.   It don't make things better to doubt profoundly whether we have any business to be at war at all.   I remember telling you at Warboys (what a good day that was!) that I deeply mistrusted Chamberlain. Since then I have been thinking worse and worse of him: I hope that I am in the wrong, but only hope.

...Then I feel a beast for lazing here in the sunshine among the Spaniards who heartily enjoy all our misfortunes.   And the worst of it is that lazing is obviously and visibly doing me good.   Really and truly the temptation comes to me, when the sky is at its bluest, to resign my professorship, realise my small fortune and become a Canario for the days that remain. On the other hand three or four projects occasionally twitch my sleeve—connected with the Selden Society, which has behaved more than handsomely by me. But both sets of motives conspire to keep me lying in the sun and saying with the Apostles "Lord! it is good for us to be here."

Well you don't laze.   I congratulate you heartily on coming out at the other end of the *Utilitarians*. You would not give me the pleasure of proof sheets— I regret it, but shall have the whole book soon and enjoyable it will be.   Especially I want to see what you say of Austin.   Since I was here I wrote an article "Hist. Engl. Law" for the *Encyclop. Britan.* and risked about Austin a couple of sentences which are not in accordance with common repute—and now I feel a little frightened. I don't want to be unjust, but I cannot see exactly where the greatness comes in. So I am curious to know your judgment about this—and many other things. I should like a long talk with you in these prehistoric surroundings.

To Frederick Pollock.

Casa Peñate, Monte,
Les Palmas.
5/2/00.

My opinions about the origin of this wretched war are not worth stating and are extremely distressing to one who holds them. It will be enough to tell you that this summer John Morley seemed to me the one English statesman who was keeping his head cool, and I have not read anything that has changed my mind. I fear that the whole affair will look bad in history. And the worst of it is that the cold fit will come with a vengeance.

We have no good news yet. I hope for some this afternoon. Your letter came by Marseilles—to my surprise, for we rarely get a mail that way. Our last tidings are of speeches made by generals and these do not cheer me. Last night I had a talk with a man who knew the Transvaal and who fears that our volunteer marksmen will not hit much until they have had two months of South African atmosphere: the unaccustomed eye makes wildly incorrect estimates of distance.

You speak of dragoons. "My period," a very short one 1558–63 is full of the "swart-rutter." The English government's one idea of carrying on a big war, if war there was to be, was that of hiring German "swart-rutters." They did much pistolling, and I suppose that you know, I don't, how big a machine was the pistol of those days. Well, the War Office temp. Mary (only there was not one) was open to criticism. Every ounce of powder that England had was imported from the Netherlands. This had to go on for a while under Elizabeth—there are amusing letters from English agents wherein "bales of cloth," and so on, have an esoteric meaning.

A starved Canarian hound has attached itself to us —of the grey-hound type, and sundry small additions are made to the menagerie as occasion serves. A parrot died yesterday—had drunk too much water, so an expert says—was called José—his fellow Juan still screams. In the neighbouring hotel is another with atrocious German habits acquired from the head waiter —will drink himself drunk with beer and swear terribly. I hear rumours of an additional monkey whose name is to be Loango.

I play schoolmaster—How they have turned the Latin grammar inside out!—and I miss my Rule of Three. In a Spanish Census paper I for once made myself "doctor iuris": Glasgow allows me to say "utriusque." I added to the population capable of reading and writing no less than five names—for our trilingual Switzer was to be included—and this will seriously affect Canarian statistics.

But I like this illiterate folk.

To Henry Jackson.

Casa Peñate, Monte,
Las Palmas.
18 *Feb.* 1900.

It is downright wickedly pleasant here. By here
I do not mean in Las Palmas—which stinketh—but
some seven miles out of it and some 1300 feet above
it, in a "finca" that we were lucky enough to hire:
that is something between a farm house and a villa.
The Spaniard of the middle class is a town-loving
animal. He likes to have up country a house to which
he can go for six weeks or so in the year and where he
keeps a major domo (= bailiff) who supplies the town
house with country produce. Such a finca we hired
for £1 a week, and there we live very comfortably and
very cheaply among vines and oranges and so forth.
Life here would have been impossible if my wife had
not acquired the Spanish, or rather the Canario, tongue
with wonderful rapidity. I fancy that some of her
language is strong; but if you want anything here you
must shout.

I am right glad to hear that it is no worse with
you. But just you be careful about cold. I know it
is the worst enemy that I have, and I suspect that you
will find the same. I have often wondered how you
contrived to live in "a thorough draught." The time
comes when one cannot do it, and that time came to
me early. In the sunshine I begin to make some flesh,
the wind no longer whistles through my ribs and I

have not had ache or pain these two months. (Interval during which the writer gets himself out of the aforesaid sunshine which to-day has an African quality.) I wish you could be here, but wonder whether you could be demoralized; some demoralization would do you good, but I cannot imagine you as lazy as I am. Still you might try. And really though I am lazy I have managed to do some things that I should not have done at home and hope to have something to offer the Press when I return. The subject of my meditations is the damnability of corporations. I rather think that they must be damned: the Chartered for example.

News as you suppose comes here fitfully. Sometimes a telegram reaches Las Palmas, and occasionally it is not contradicted. But in the main we depend upon newspapers. I feel somewhat of a beast for being outside all this war trouble, more especially as I went abroad with a very low opinion of the Government's South African policy. That opinion I should like to change but I cannot. Your amateur strategist must be pretty intolerable. I have met a few people here who knew something of the Transvaal and they have none of them been cheerful. The puzzle to me "after the event" is why more was not known in Downing Street. I can't help fearing that when all comes out the whole affair will look very bad....

It will be a very strange book that *History* of ours[1]. I am extremely curious to see whether Acton will be able to maintain a decent amount of harmony among the chapters. Some chapters that I saw did not look much like parts of one and the same book.

[1] *The Cambridge Modern History.*

Before I went off I put my chapter into his lordship's hands. I never was more relieved than when I got rid of it. His lordship's lordship was considerate to an invalid and only excepted to a few new words that I had made, but I daresay he swore—if he ever swears —in private.... I never knew time run as it runs here. Soon I shall have to be thinking of my return with the mixedest feelings. I am going to give Cambridge a last chance. If it cannot keep me at about 9 stone, I shall "realise" such patrimony as I have and buy a finca. Then for the great treatise De Damnabilitate Universitatis.

To HENRY JACKSON.

CASA PEÑATE, MONTE,
LAS PALMAS.
12*th January*, 1901.

It was very good of you to give me a piece of your New Year's Eve and to tell me much that I wanted to know. For my part I am practising the art of writing while lying flat on my back and am flattering myself that I make some progress, though the management of a pipe complicates the matter. The result of lying abed is that I am getting through much too quickly the small store of books that I brought with me and am falling back on the resources of the one bookshop that the island contains. If this sort of thing goes on I shall be driven to Spanish translations of Zola. I have just finished Feuillet's *La Muerta*—but then

I knew the French original. After what you say I must see whether Erckmann-Chatrian has been done into Spanish. In a list that I have before me I see Dickens down for "Dias penosos" and some Wilkie Collins—but apparently the novel-reading Spaniard lives for the most part on Frenchmen, especially Zola. I shall never talk Spanish. I believe that what is or used to be called a classical education makes many cowards : the dread of " howlers " keeps me silent when I ought to plunge regardless of consequences.

I fancy that the comparison that you instituted between the life of the Roman and the life of the Spaniard as seen by me in these islands might be extended to a good many particulars. When, as happens for about eleven months in the year, you are not living at your finca, you occasionally pay it visits with a party of friends—male friends only— whom you entertain there. You eat a great deal and drink until you are merry—then late in the evening you drive back to town twanging a guitar, and, if you can, you sing inane verses made impromptu. Our landlord had one of these carouses the day before he handed over the house to us, and my wife's account of the state in which the house was when she entered and set some servants to scrub it is not for publication....Is not this rather classical ?

To Frederick Pollock.

Casa Peñate, Monte.
21 *Jan.* 1901.

Also I wonder what has gone wrong with the mails—we might be at the other end of the earth, so slow is news to reach us. A rumour came up yesterday from the ciudad which makes me reflect that I don't know for certain whether you have a queen in England or a king. And I can't go and see how all this is, for if I leave my bed, I am soon sent back there again by this blameworthy neuralgia which threatens to become what Glanvill calls morbus reseantisae. Et sic iaceo discinctus discalciatus et sine braccis ut patuit militibus comitatus qui missi fuerunt ad me videndum et qui michi dederunt diem apud Turrim Lundoniae in quindena Pasche.

So I make some progress through Spanish novels— or rather novels that have been translated into Spanish. At present I am in *Resurreccion* by the Conde Leon Tolstoy —which is easy. I find Perez Galdos a little too hard for my recumbent position, and dictionaries are bad bed-fellows. I have been indolently making for subsequent use a sort of Year Book grammar. I have got a pretty complete être and avoir—and really I think that the lawyers had a fair command of all the tenses—I have seen some well sustained subjunctives.

You spoke of Maine. Well, I always talk of him with reluctance, for on the few occasions on which I sought to verify his statements of fact I came to the conclusion that he trusted much to a memory that played him tricks and rarely looked back at a book that he had once read: e.g. his story about the position of the half-blood in the Law of Normandy seems to me a mere dream that is contradicted by every version of the custumal.

By the way, when you discoursed of the term "comparative Jurisprudence," had you noticed that Austin used it? I was surprised by seeing it in his book the other day. Burgenses de Cantebrige dederunt michi libertatem burgi sui honoris causa quia edidi cartas suas. Gratificatus Sum.

To John C. Gray,

Professor of Law in the University of Harvard.

Downing College, Cambridge.

21 *April*, 1901.

My best thanks for *Future Interests in Personal Property*, which has just come to my hands on my return from the Canaries. For a few days my interest in it must be future, but will be vested, indefeasible, real and not impersonal.

Yours in perpetuity,

(Signed)   F. W. Maitland.

To Henry Jackson.

5 Leon y Castillo,
Telde,
Gran Canaria.
30 *December*, 1901.

Here I am lying in the sun which shines as if it were June and not December. This year our "finca" is in the midst of a "pueblo." The front of our house faces a high street which is none too clean—but then you keep the front of your house so shut up that you see nothing of the street and at the back all is orange and coffee and banana and so forth. Telde is the centre of an important trade in tomatos—the whole village is employed in the work of packing them for the English market and sending them off to the shops in Las Palmas. Really it has become a very big industry in these last years and if English people gave up eating tomatos, hundreds of Canarios would be in a bad way. But there! You don't want to hear of foreign parts, and if we could meet our talk would be of Cambridge....

I am told that I have been put back into the Press Syndicate. I do not refuse and shall be very glad if in any way I can further the interests of the big history. The first volume is with me and I enjoy it.

To Leslie Stephen.

5, Leon y Castillo,
Telde,
Las Palmas,
Gran Canaria.
20 Jan. 1902.

I was glad of your letter.   I had been in a poor way and it cheered me.   Now I am doing well and ride a bit on my cycle along one of the three roads of the island.   I thought that you would like *Joh. Althusius* if you could penetrate the shell[1].   I like all that man's books, and his history of things in general as seen from the point of view of a student of corporations is full of good stuff, besides being to all appearance appallingly learned.   I rather fancy that Hobbes's political feat consisted in giving a new twist to some well worn theories of the juristic order and then inventing a psychology which would justify that twist.   I shall be very much interested to hear what you have to say about the old gentleman.   A many years ago I saw in the Museum a copy of the *Leviathan* with a note telling how the wretched old atheist was buried head downwards or face downwards or something of the sort in a garden—a nice little legend in the making !

Have you read *De Mirabilibus Pecci* ?   Stevenson the Anglo-Saxon scholar, who travelled outwards with me, told me that the first recorded appearance of the

---

[1] Otto Gierke's monograph on Johannes Althusius, published 1880.

name of the Peak (something like Pecesus) shows that
the great cavern was called after the Devil's hinder
parts. Did Hobbes know that ? What a thing it is
to be a philologer !

To LESLIE STEPHEN.

5, LEON Y CASTILLO
TELDE,
GRAN CAN. RIA.
30 *Jan.* 1902.

Let me wish you a happy new year and then ask
for a line in return. It doesn't follow in law or in fact
that because I have nothing to say that you care to
hear therefore you have nothing to say that I care to
hear. Q.E.D.

Why did you make my life miserable by suggesting
that grammar does not allow me to wish you a happy
new year and does not allow you to send me a letter ?
I consulted a professed grammarian who told me
that " me " and " you " are good datives and " to " in
such cases an unnecessary and historically unjustifiable
preposition. Go on like this and you will end where
the Spaniard is, and he loves " to " his parents, etc.
When we still have to contend with relics of a subjunctive you need not be making more difficulties.
I am led into these exceedingly uninteresting remarks
by the nature of my only pursuit. I had a bad time
on the voyage. Something went wrong with my works
and since I have been here I have not had much
choice between lying almost flat and suffering a good

deal of pain. So I have been copying Year Books from the manuscripts that I brought from Cambridge and since the scribes did not finish their words and I have to supply the endings I have been compelled to take a serious interest in old French Grammar. However, things are improving. I had ten minutes on the cycle yesterday and hope soon to see a little of the country. We are in a village this year. It is the centre of the trade in tomatos. Boxes of tomatos with the Telde mark have been seen even in the Cambridge market place. As I lie here I am surrounded by oranges, coffee, bananas, etc., and we have even a true dragon tree. It is wonderfully beautiful. Florence and the children are exceedingly happy and I am beginning to doubt whether I shall get them back to Cambridge when the Spring comes. You would think that Florence had never talked anything but Spanish. Not that I would warrant its Castilian quality, but at any rate it is rapid and highly effectual.

To Henry Jackson.

5, Leon y Castillo,
Telde,
Gran Canaria.
1st February, 1902.

I am sorry indeed that the part of your letter to which I looked anxiously contained such bad news—and having said that I think that I won't say more —it is so useless.

The Spaniard ends his letter with S.S.S.Q.B.S.M. and I understand this to mean su seguro servidor que besa sus manos—but he puts it in even when he writes to the papers and there is no thought of any real kissing in the case. I send you two little bits of English for (!) decipherment. They appear day by day and month by month in the *Diario de Las Palmas* and I hope that they are intelligible to its non-English readers. The said newspaper is one of some half dozen daily rags published in our "ciudad"—I am surprised by their number. They seem largely to live upon ancient English papers—I mean papers which have taken a week to get here and have then been lying about in the hotels for another week or more. Hence queer snips from *Tit Bits*, etc.

Which makes me think of Acton. (His professed admiration of *Tit Bits* has some basis in fact : at least I once entered a railway carriage and found him deep in said paper.) What a prodigious catechism he addressed to you! I should like to have seen your reply....Many thanks for news of the *History*. I hope that all will go well now : I think that the team looks strong. I hear that I am to serve on the Press Syndicate : I doubt I shall do much good there—still I am quite willing to hear others talk and shall be interested in all that concerns the big book.

These last weeks I have been doing splendidly and have got through a spell of copying which would never have been done had I stayed in England—as you say, life in Cambridge is an interruption. Buckland is a good companion and I think that we have taken our cycles where cycles have not been before—a crowd of ragged boys pursues—"chiquillos" convinced of our insanity.

If you have good news to give, give it.

To John C. Gray.

DOWNING COLLEGE,
CAMBRIDGE.
19 *April,* 1902.

I returned yesterday from a winter spent in the Canaries where I am compelled to take refuge. Already I have read your article about gifts for non-charitable purposes and have been delighted by it. It puts an accent on what I think a matter of great historical importance—namely the extreme liberality of our law about charitable trusts. It seems to me that our people slid unconsciously from the enforcement of the rights of a c.q.t. to the establishment of trusts without a c.q.t. —the so-called charitable trusts: and I think that continental law shows that this was a step that would not and could not be taken by men whose heads were full of Roman Law. *Practically* the private man who creates a charitable trust does something that is very like the creation of an artificial person, and does it without asking leave of the State.

I only saw Thayer for a few hours, but I feel his death as the death of a friend. The loss must be deeply felt at Harvard.

To Henry Jackson.

DOWNING.
6 *July,* 1902.

You repay me my letter with usurious interest. However you are *sui juris*—or ought I to say *tui* ?— and I doubt a court of equity would extend to you the protection which it bestows on improvident young gentlemen.

No I had nothing to write of Acton. A few memorable talks on Sunday afternoons were all I had. To my great regret I did not hear the first of the Eranus papers....What the literary Nachlass is like I cannot tell and am not likely to know. I saw the notes for an introductory chapter[1] confided to Figgis. They seemed to me to be quite useless in the hands of anyone save him who made them. They struck me as very sad : the notes of a man who could not bring to the birth the multitude of thoughts that were crowding in his mind.

Have you seen Sidgwick's small book on philosophy? I think it in some respects the most Sidgwickian thing that is in print. I can hear most of it—some of it from the hearth-rug or at the Eranus.

I think that the K.C.B. came to Stephen just at the right moment and that he is really pleased by it. About his condition I don't know the exact truth. The good thing is that there is little discomfort. He is writing Ford Lectures for Oxford, but says that he will not be able to deliver them. Have you seen in his *George Eliot* the remark about Edmund Gurney ? " I have always fancied—though without any evidence, that some touches in Deronda were drawn from one of her friends, Edmund Gurney a man of remarkable charm of character and as good-looking as Deronda" (p. 191). What think you ?

[1] To the *Cambridge Modern History.*

To Henry Jackson.

Muy Señor mio

Deseo que pase Vd. bien las Pascuas y que tenga feliz año nuevo
Quedo de Vd. atento y Seguro
Servidor que besa su mano

F. W. Maitland.

From an exercise on the use of the subjunctive. Beyond this point my Spanish will not carry me. Compulsory Greek, acting on a fine natural stupidity, deprived me early of all power of learning languages. I envy my children who chatter to the servants in what is good enough Canario, though I doubt it being Castilian. My voyage was abominable. I am driven into the second class. I like second class *men* (not women): they are often very interesting people who have seen odd things and been in strange places—but a cabin close to the screw is bad and sleep was out of the question. Two lines of F. Myers (have I got them rightly) got into my head and set themselves to the accompanying noises:—"doubting if any recompense hereafter waits to atone the intolerable wrong?" But this was faithlessness—it is all atoned by a few hours of this glorious sunshine. Already I am regenerate and a new man.... Do you know Paul Bourget's *L'Étape*? It is not great but it served to kill some bad hours. And do you know Huysman? He looks to me like a debauchee who has turned himself into a ritualistic curate and is very sweet upon his highly artificial style. I am now tackling *Gil Blas* in the classical Spanish translation which some say is better than the original.

My house of call is Quiney's but I am up country at a place called Tafira.

CASA VERDA,
TAFIRA.
17 *Jan.* 1903.

Your letter about Paris is to hand. Well I envy you. Yours are the joys that I should have liked if I had my choice—but I must not complain, for I am having a superlatively good time. I don't exactly know why it is but the sun makes all the difference to me—I live here and don't live in England. I am even beginning to boast of my powers as a hill rider : but if ever I come here again I shall bring a machine with a very low gear and a free wheel: that is what you want if you live half way up a road that rises pretty steadily for 21 kilometres to 2600 feet. My friend Bennett who has vast experience recommends a gear of 50 for such work.

Meanwhile I push on with the Year Books. My first volume is done in the rough and a good piece is in print. Being away from books I become intrigued in small verbal problems. Am now observing the liberal use of the verb *lier*. In French you (an advocate) are said to *lier* the seisin, or the esplees, or

the like, in this person or that. When translating I
naturally write "lay," and I have a suspicion that the
"to lay" of our legal vocabulary (e.g. to lay these
damages) really descends from lier—que piensa V^d?
That is the sort of triviality that occupies my mind :—
however I am meditating a final say about the personality of states and corporations. Why not bring over
Salmond to succeed you at Oxford? He is a good
man. Local politics are interesting. I think that
when Gladstone was in power he never was subjected
to such continuous assaults as are directed against the
Alcalde of Las Palmas by the organ of opinion that I
patronize. Drought and flood, mud and dust, small-
pox and measles are all from him, he fills the butchers'
shops with large blue flies. But I should like to hear
the lectures that you make for los Yanquis (N.B. in a
Spanish mouth Americano is apt to mean a Spanish
speaking man—and Yanqui is not uncivilly meant).

Much rain has fallen—but a road recovers from
the most appalling mud in a very few hours.

TO LESLIE STEPHEN.

CASA VERDA,
TAFIRA.

17 *Jan.* 1903.

The news that we get of you out here is satis-
factory rather than satisfying—I mean that we have
heard little, but it was all to the good. The last
intelligence takes you back to your home and I feel
good reason for hoping that long before now you have

become reasonably comfortable. What I wish you know.

All here goes well. I am having a supremely good time—the only pains are those given by my conscience or by the voice that exists where my conscience should be—but the remedies for moral twinges are not difficult to come by in this world of sin—which also is (locally) a world of corrupting sunshine.

I brought with me this time all the three supplementary volumes of *Dict. Natl. Biog.* I stare at them and wonder how anybody can have the energy to make such things. Even novels strike me as laborious productions when the sun is at its best.

We have been having rain: and when it rains here you find that the roof of your house has been surprised by the performance. I am now engaged in drying a boxful of copied Year Book which unfortunately was left beneath a weak point in the ceiling. Is it "ceiling" by the way? I don't know, and while I am in the garden the dictionary is in the house and I don't care a perrita (primarily little bitch but also a five centimo piece) how this or any other word spells itself; and all this I ascribe to the sun.

It will be a good day when I get a postcard signed L. S.—but don't be in a hurry to send one before the spirit moves you.

Back at Hobbes again? I hope so. Florence joins me in hopes—as you can well suppose.

Yours very affectionately,

F. W. MAITLAND.

To Henry Jackson.

Tafira,
Las Palmas.
14 *February*, 1903.

We have been having bad news of sorts from home and this has spoilt what would otherwise have been a pleasant time, for though we have had heavy rain— even snow on the hill tops—we keep a really working sun that is up to a sun's business and converts the most appalling mud into dust in the space of a few hours. Until just lately I have been wondrous well. My amusement I have taken in the shape of lessons in Spanish from the hostess of the village inn. She prides herself on not talking like the other folk of Tafira—but asked me whether Perez Galdos wrote *Gil Blas*. P. G. is by birth a Canario and mighty proud they are of him here. Every little town has a street named after him. To my mind he is a most unequal storyteller—sometimes very good, at others dull.

To Frederick Pollock.

Tafira.
14 *March*, 1903.

...Did I tell you that a while ago I was informed that I had been elected a bencher of Lincoln's Inn (with the "usual fees" forgiven). The news made my hair stand on end—one of the vacant bishoprics would have been less of a surprise.

To A. W. Verrall.

Quiney's Hotel,
Las Palmas.
14 *Feb.* 1903.

Until just this week I have been doing wonderfully well. Now the messenger of Satan has returned to buffet me and abate my pride. So the cycle has to rest; but I am hopeful that the visitation may be short—it ought to be if the climate has anything to do with the matter, for after some rainy weeks we are on the sun again. El Señor Cura "clapped in the prayer for rain" so very effectually that he had to protest before all saints that he had not meant quite so much as all that. Rainmaking is still one of the chief duties of the priesthood in such a country as this.

The proposal made by "the minister" and mentioned by you was rejected by return of post[1]. There were seven or eight good causes for the refusal—all of which will at once occur to your l'dship except perhaps one which I will tell you. My present place has been made extremely easy to me by the very great kindness of such colleagues as it has happened to few to have. Even if I had been a historian and an able-bodied man I should have thought many times before I changed my estate.—And what you say of the crowd at Bury's first lecture—I thought the appointment very

---

[1] Maitland was invited to succeed Lord Acton in the Chair of Modern History at Cambridge.

good—confirms my view. The Regius Professor of
Modern History is expected to speak to the world at
large and even if I had anything to say to the W.
at L. I don't think that I should like full houses and
the limelight. So I go back to the Year Books.
Really they are astonishing. I copy and translate for
some hours every day and shall only have scratched
the surface if I live to the age of Methusalem—but if I
last a year or two longer I shall be a "dab" at real
actions. It was a wonderful game as intricate as chess
and not like chess cosmopolitan. Unravelling it is an
amusement not unlike that of turning the insides out
of ancient comedies I guess.

To W. W. Buckland.

Telde.

14 *Feb.* 1903.

Muy estimado colega y querido amigo mío

Espero que Vᵈ no ha olvidado lo que ha
aprendido de la lengua castillana cuando estaba en Gran
Canaria el año próximo pasado. Por tanto me esforzaré
escribir una carta en aquel lenguaje aunque no puedo
expresar mis pensamientos sin muchas disparates ridicu-
losas que quizas Vᵈ perdonará.

Mientras las primeras semanas de mia estancia en
Tafira hacia buen tiempo y D. Benito del Colegio de
Manuel y yo dabamos algunos largos paseos en nuestras
bicicletas. Despues de su partida en Enero llovía
muchas veces y se ha visto nieve en las cumbres.

Los barrancos fueron llenos de agua y le agua se introdujó por el tejado de nuestra casa. El fango me recordaba el viaje que hicimos en Marzo de Galdar á Telde. No mé gustaba el frio y no estoy tan bién que estaba hace poco tiempo. Mi antiguo enemigo me amenaza pero espero que le venceré. De consiguiente no he ido á Telde; pero espero ir luego, y si fuere buscaré á Santiago su criado de V^d y le daré el duro que mi dió para él. La viruela todavia se enfurece en Telde y en las Palmas tambien.

Todos sus amigos de V^d estan muy bien pero un señor cuyo nombre no mencionaré estaba fuertemente ébrio cuando le ví la ultima vez....

Quiero leer el libro de Sen. X aunque no sé si le podré entender. Es un hombre docto, doctísimo pero stogioso—esta ultima no puedo deletrear.

Estas pocas palabras son una recompensa muy ligera por su carta de V^d que me interesó mucho y por que estoy muy agradecido pero he tomado un largo tiempo escribiendolas. Si pudiere[1] escribir mas facilmente le contaría a V^d todos los sucesos que han acontecido en Gran Canaria. Pero es preciso acabar.

Con muchas memorias

Quedo su afectuoso amigo

F. W. MAITLAND.

Al muy excelente

Sen. D. G. G. BUCKLAND.

[1] Mire V^d! No verá cada día el condicional de subjunctivo.

To John C. Gray.

Downing College,
Cambridge.
4 *Oct.* 1903.

I should like to take this opportunity of asking
you a question which you will be able to answer very
easily.   In 1862 our Parliament made it possible for
any seven or more persons associated for any lawful
purpose to form themselves into a corporation.   But
this provision was accompanied by a prohibition.   For
the future the formation of large partnerships (of more
than 20 persons) was forbidden.   In effect the legislature said that every big association having for its object
the acquisition of gain must be a corporation.   Thereby
the formation of "unincorporated joint stock companies"
was stopped.   I may say in passing that now-a-days
few Englishmen are aware of the existence of this
prohibitory law because the corporate form has proved
itself to be very much more convenient than the unincorporate.   Now what I should like to know is
whether when in your States the time came for general
corporation laws there was any parallel legislation
against unincorporated companies.   I have some of
your American books on Corporations and I gather
from them that the repressive or prohibitory side of
our Companies Act is not represented among you.
But am I right in drawing this inference, and (if so)
should I also be right in supposing that you would
see constitutional objections to such a rule as that of

which I am speaking : i.e. a rule prohibiting the formation of large partnerships or unincorporated joint-stock companies ? A friend in New York supplied me with some very interesting trust deeds which in effect seemed to create companies of this sort. Should I then be right in supposing that in the U.S.A. the unincorporate company lived on beside the new trading corporation ?

I am endeavouring to explain in a German journal how our law (or equity) of trusts enabled us to keep alive "unincorporate bodies" which elsewhere must have perished. Of course I must not speak of America. Still I should like to know in a general way whether the development of the "unincorporated company" which we repressed in 1862 was similarly repressed in the States, and a word or two from you about this matter would be most thankfully received.

By the way—and here I enter your own particular close—I observed that those New York deeds were careful to confine the trust within the limits of the perpetuity rule. Is it settled American law that this is necessary ? We explain our *clubs* by saying that as the whole equitable ownership is vested in the original members there can be no talk of perpetuity— and I believe that there are some extremely important unincorporated companies with transferable shares (formed before 1862—in particular the London Stock Exchange) which are built up on this theory : the theory is that the original shareholders were in equity absolute masters of the land, buildings, etc. Does that commend itself to you ?

There! you see what comes of writing to me! A

whole catechism! Please think no more of it unless a very few words would set my feet in the straight road.

Most of my time is being given to the Year Books. The first volume is with the binder.

I often look back with great pleasure to the few hours that you and Mrs Gray spent with us in Gloucestershire. Would that I could see you again, but all my journeys have to be to the Canaries.

To JOHN C. GRAY.

DOWNING COLLEGE,
CAMBRIDGE.
15 *Nov.* 1903.

Your very kind letter of the 4th is exactly what I wanted. But surely there is nothing "odd" in my asking you questions which you of living men can answer best. It would be odd if I went elsewhere.

The brief in Howe *v.* Morse is extremely interesting. I think that an English Court would take your view in such a case, but when it comes to questions about legacies our judges sometimes *say* things which stray from the path of rectitude as drawn by Prof. Gray.

I have been trying all this summer to finish an essay designed to explain to Germans the nature of a trust, and especially the manner in which the trust enabled us to keep alive all sorts of "bodies" which were not technically corporate. I am obliged now to flee to the Canaries leaving this unfinished, for a particularly fraudulent summer has made me very useless. Some one ought to explain our trust to the world at large, for I am inclined to think that the construction thereof is the greatest feat that men of our race have performed in the field of jurisprudence. Whether I shall be able to do this remains to be seen—but it ought to be done.

To Leslie Stephen.

Leon y Castillo 5,
Telde,
Gran Canaria.
6 *Dec.* 1903.

I fear that I must not carry my good wishes beyond the point of hoping that the improvement that I saw last time I visited you has gone further and that at any rate you are easy and free from pain. I have just had a week in this island. Part of it I spent foolishly in bed but now I am in a delightful atmosphere and have been thoroughly enjoying your Hobbes. It is worthy of you, and you know what I mean when I say that. I have been all through it once and have corrected most of the typist's errors. A few little points must stand over until I can command the whole of the "Works" (I only brought two volumes with me) but they are not of such a kind as would prevent the copy going to the printers, and I propose to send it to them very soon, for they will let me keep the stuff in type until I am again in England. The difficulties to which I refer are words occurring in your quotations from Hobbes—just here and there your writing beats me, but a few minutes with Molesworth will settle the matter....

I think I told you that in my estimate you have written, more rather than less, your due tale of words. I shall add nothing save some tag which will serve as a substitute for the missing end of the final paragraph (said tag I may be able to submit to you) and I shall omit nothing save trifles unless the publishers insist.

I have been speculating as to what T. H. would have said had he lived until 1688. If it becomes clear that your "sovereign" is going to acknowledge the pope's claims, this of course is no breach of any contract between ruler and ruled (for there is no such contract) but is there not an abdication? Putting theory out of the question, which would the old gentleman have disliked most, Revolution against Leviathan, or a Leviathan with the Roman fisherman's hook in his nose?

Well he was a delightful old person and deserved the expositor whom he has found.

To Henry Jackson.

Leon y Castillo 5,
Telde,
Gran Canaria.
13 *December*, 1903.

This may—I cannot be sure that it will—be in time to salute you on Christmas day. Posts are irregular and nine miles of bad road separate us from

Las Palmas. So, not being able as yet to cycle to our ciudad, I shall just drop this into the village letter box and trust that it may reach you some day.

I had the good luck to find the Bay of Biscay reflecting a really warm sun and very soon I could hardly believe that so grey a place as Cambridge existed. I arrived here at the end of a prolonged drought and the good folk of Telde "clapped on the prayer for rain": or rather they did much more; they carried round the town a milagroso Cristo whom they keep for great occasions. I am not sure that the priest let him go his rounds until he, the priest, saw that the clouds were collecting thick over the mountains. Anyhow the rain came at once, to the great edification of the faithful. Since then we have celebrated the Immaculate Conception. It is very queer how events get turned into persons. The Conception became a person for the people. I think that the historian of myths would learn a good deal here. Just lately I discovered—it was no great discovery—that the pet name "Concha" is the short for Concepcion, as Lola is the short for Dolores. My protestant mind has been a little shocked by a female form of Jesus, namely "Jesusa."

I am living in hope that Pollock's successor at Oxford may be Vinogradoff. I wish much that we had him at Cambridge.

I am curious to hear any news that there may be concerning the deliberations of the great syndicate. I suppose that something will be known before I return to Cambridge—if ever I return. I say "if ever" for I am always thinking of resignation. Out

here I can do a great deal with photographed manuscripts and so on, whereas in England I get nothing
done.

You I suppose are deep in "Josephism"—by the
way has anybody endeavoured to transfer that term
from a manner of treating the church to Mr C.'s fiscal
policy ? My latest newspaper gives the Duke's oration
—how very good our Chancellor can be!—but no doubt
that is with you a very ancient history[1]. My own impression when I left England was that the crusade was
failing.

To Henry Jackson.

Leon y Castillo 5,
Telde,
Gran Canaria.
14 *Feb.* 1904.

No, you draw a wrong inference from my silence.
When I am hurt I cry. When I am not crying I am
happy. In this instance I have been very happy
indeed and so busy that I have taken six weeks over
a novel, and am once more developing a corn on my
little finger by copying....All that you tell me of the
Studies Syndicate is extremely interesting—you may
rely upon my discretion, for as you remark there is
nobody to whom I could babble—even *La Manana*
which is often hard up for news would I fear give me
nothing for secret intelligence concerning the S.S.

[1] The Duke of Devonshire, Chancellor of the University of
Cambridge, had criticised Mr Joseph Chamberlain's fiscal proposals.

Writing those initials made me think of your
Eranus. I wish that I had heard you. I think that
I might have been able to add an ancient story or
two. I think that I once told you how the "to wit"
placed after the name of a county at the beginning of
a legal record (e.g. Cambridgeshire, to wit, A.B. com-
plains that C. D. etc.) represents a mere flourish Ϟ
dividing the name of the county from the beginning
of the story. This was mistaken for a long S which
was supposed to be the abbreviation of scilicet. The
Spaniards are fond of using mere initials : after a dead
person's name you can put q.d.h.e.g. = que Dios haya
en gloria. The case that amuses me most is that you
can speak of the Host as S.D.M. (his divine majesty—
just like H.R.H.). One day in Las Palmas I had to
spring from my bicycle and kneel in the road because
S.D.M. was coming along. But I have just had my
revenge. I have been mistaken for S.D.M. They
ring a little bell in front of him. I rarely ring my
bicycle bell because I don't think it a civil thing to do
in a land where cycles are very rare. However the
other day I was almost upon the backs of two men, so
I rang. They started round and at the same time
instinctively raised their hats—and instead of S.D.M.
there was only an *hereje*.

To be sure those letters of Acton's are thrilling.
I saw them out here last year. Mrs Drew wanted
me to edit them. I declined the task, after talking to
Leslie Stephen. Obviously I was not the right man.
I am boundlessly ignorant of contemporary history
and could not in the least tell what would give un-
deserved and unnecessary pain. On the other hand

I should think that H. Paul was the right man for the job.

...I hope that Vol. III is doing well, though I foresee that I shall be slated in all quarters. Acton was an adroit flatterer and induced me to put my hand far into a very nest of hornets.

To A. W. Verrall.

C/o Leacock & Co.
Funchal,
Madeira.
15 *Jan.* 1905.

It is good to see your hand and kind of you to write to me, especially as I fear that writing is not so easy to you as it once was. I do very earnestly hope that things go fairly well with you and that you have not much pain. Yesterday I was thinking a lot of your courage and my cowardice for I took an off day—off from the biography I mean—and attained an altitude of (say) 5250 feet (a cog-wheel railway saving me 2000 thereof, however) and I was bounding about up there like a kid of the goats—and very base I thought myself not to be lecturing. There is not much left of me avoirdupoisly speaking; but that little bounds along when it has had a good sunning; and today I have a rubbed heel and a permanent thirst as in the good old days. Missing a train on said railway I made the last part of the descent in the special Madeira fashion on a sledge glissading down over polished cobble stone pavement—a youth running behind to hold the thing back by a rope : it gives the unaccustomed a pretty little squirm at starting. Up in the hills it is a pleasant world—you pass through many different zones of vegetation very rapidly—at one moment all is laurel and heath—you cross a well-marked line and all is tilling—then you are out among dead bracken on an open hill-top that might be English. Get on a sledge and wiss (or is it wiz?) you go down to the sugar and bananas through bignonia and bougain-villia which blind you by their ferocity.

To Henry Jackson.

> Leon y Castillo, 5,
> Telde,
> Gran Canaria.
> 15 *January*, 1906.

I have your second letter, not your first. The first may be lying in the Hotel at Las Palmas and I must attempt to get it. This year it is difficult to communicate with the "ciudad" for there has been a prolonged drought and the roads—but did you ever try cycling across a ploughed field? Moreover people here are lazy and casual and the semi-hispanised English people who keep the English hotels are perhaps more casual than the true Jack Spaniards. Well, I must get that letter, for which I thank in advance, even if it costs me a day's labour and some strong language. Meanwhile I will talk of canary birds. The birds are named after our islands. What our islands are named after, nobody, so I am told, knows for certain. Whether the

birds are found wild in all the seven islands I don't
know.   Certainly there are many in Gran Canaria.
Also there are many in Madeira.   The wild canary is,
I believe, always a dusky little chap, brown and green.
The sulphur coloured or canary-coloured canary is, I am
told, a work of art, and I have heard say that he was
made at Norwich : by "made" of course I mean bred
by human selection.   The most highly priced canaries
are, I believe, made in Germany.   I have known two
guineas asked for a "Hartz Mountain Canary" : it
sang *pp.* like a very sweet musical box.   On the other
hand, wild canaries are cheap here, especially if you go
up country and buy of the boys who catch them.   My
wife quotes as a fair range of price half a peseta to a
peseta and a half.   The peseta ought to be equivalent
to the franc but is much depreciated.   So let us say
that a bird can be had for a shilling.   My wife adds
that she would be very happy to import birds for your
daughter—and this is not a civil phrase but gospel
truth : she is never happier than when she is acquiring
pets as principal or agent :—so it is, and I can't help it.
I like the song of these dusky birds : it is not nearly
so piercing as that of the Norwich variety.   I daresay
that I have told you some untruths in this ornithological
excursus—but at any rate I make no mistake about the
price of wild birds or about my wife's willingness—
I might say eagerness—to transact business.

XI.

One of the principal subjects which engaged
Maitland's mind during these years was the history
of the Corporation. Problems connected with the
growth and definition of the Corporate idea had furnished the theme of the Ford Lectures and a course
upon the Corporation in English law was delivered
in Cambridge in the Autumn Term of 1899. It was
a subject from which Maitland derived deep and
peculiar delight. It brought into play the full range
of his faculties, for it was at once metaphysical, legal
and historical. It was associated with the enquiries
which he had already been making into municipal
origins, and into the law of the medieval Church, while,
at the same time, it was connected with some living
and familiar developments of modern law, with those
corporate groups which, during the later half of the
nineteenth century "had been multiplying all the world
over at a rate far outstripping the increase of natural
persons." Trades unions and joint-stock companies,
chartered boroughs and medieval universities, village
communities and townships, merchant guilds and crafts,
every form of association known to medieval or modern
life came within his view, as illustrating the way in
which Englishmen attempted "to distinguish and re-
concile the manyness of the members and the oneness

of the body." An enquiry of this kind was something entirely new in England. Here lawyers had accepted from the Canonists the view that the Corporation was a fiction of the law created by the authoritative act of the State. A mindless thing, "incapable of knowing, intending, willing, acting, distinct from the living corporators who are called its members," the Corporation is and must be the creature of the State. "Into its nostrils the State must breathe the breath of fictitious life, for otherwise it would be no animated body but individualistic dust." *Solus princeps fingit quod in rei veritate non est.* Such a theory was, as Maitland pointed out, likely to play into the hands of the paternal despot. The Corporation so conceived—and this is how not only Savigny but Blackstone also conceived it—was no subject for liberties and franchises and rights of self-government. It was but "a wheel in the State machinery." And yet in England, where the Concession theory of the Corporation was received without challenge, there had certainly not been less of autonomy and free grouping in guilds and fellowships than elsewhere. The secret of this apparent contradiction, between a theory which made corporateness the creature of a sovereign authority and a practice which enabled permanent groups to be freely formed without such authority, was to be found in a legal conception peculiar to England, the conception of the Trust. "Behind the screen of trustees and concealed from the direct scrutiny of legal theories, all manner of groups can flourish: Lincoln's Inn, or Lloyds, or the Stock Exchange, or the Jockey Club, a whole presbyterian system or even the Church of Rome

with the Pope at its head...." Even a large company,
trading with a joint-stock with vendible shares and
a handsome measure of "limited liability," could be
constructed by means of a trust deed without any
incorporation. Aided by this "loose trust-concept,"
under the shelter of which organic groups of the most
various kinds could live and prosper, English lawyers
were not vitally concerned with the theory of the
Corporation. The law of the Corporation was only
one part, and probably not the most important part, of
the English fellowship-law, but in Germany, where
no such convenient shelter had been provided for
the "unincorporate body," the case was different, and
active discussion had raged round the nature of the
Corporation. The fiction theory invented by Sinibald
Fieschi, who became Pope Innocent IV in 1243, and
developed and expounded by Savigny, had proved
itself inadequate in an age of joint-stock companies
and railway collisions; and in the rising tide of German
nationalism men were prone to question the validity of
a conception derived from the alien jurisprudence of
Rome. A new school of thinkers arose preaching the
theory of the Genossenschaft or Fellowship. They
held that the German Fellowship was neither fictitious
nor State-made, that it was ".a living organism, and a
real person with body and members and will of its
own," a group-person with a group-will. The most
important representative of this new school of German
realists was Dr Gierke, whose work Maitland introduced to the British public after his first winter exile
in Grand Canary.

Maitland had followed with unflagging interest and

steady enthusiasm the great outburst of legal literature in Germany which preceded the construction of the German Civil Code. Of the Code itself he wrote that "it was the most carefully considered statement of a nation's law that the world has ever seen"; while he found in the legal debate of the Germanist and Romanist schools work which sometimes showed "a delicacy of touch and a subtlety of historical perception," of which Englishmen, "having no pressing need for comparison," could know little. For the purpose which Maitland had in view, the explanation of the way in which Englishmen had conceived of group life in its various embodiments, this subtle and delicate treatment of the forms of legal thought, this "ideal morphology" of the Germans, was no less full of suggestion than the ample historical science with which it was supported. It provided tests, and suggested those points of analogy and contrast between English and German development, which give to Maitland's treatment of the Corporate and Unincorporate Body the quality of an original discourse upon the legal and political theory of Western Europe.

Nor was the interest of the subject merely speculative. Maitland was a practical lawyer with a genius for detecting the source of bad law and bad administration in confused modes of thinking about ultimate questions. Looking for the moment at the English law concerning Corporations through the spectacles of a German realist, he detected as the principal offence against jurisprudence "a certain half-heartedness in our treatment of unincorporate groups." We were unwilling to recognise trades-unions for example as

persons, while we made fairly adequate provision for
their continuous life. The consequence of this half-
heartedness was felt in the domain of public administration as well as in the domain of private law.
Englishmen had accepted "a bad and foreign theory,
which coupling corporateness with princely privilege
refused to recognise and call forth into vigour the
bodiliness that was immanent in every township."
The Americans had been less pedantic and had permitted the New England town to develop its inherent
corporateness. We, on the contrary, influenced by the
Concession theory of the Corporation, had shrunk
from declaring the village to be a legal person, the
subject of rights and the object of gifts. The consequences of this fatal blunder were not measurable
merely in terms of administrative symmetry; but so
measured they were very great. No one knew better
than Maitland the "appalling mess" of English local
government. He had described its broader features
in *Justice and Police*; he analysed certain underlying
sources of confusion in *Township and Borough*. In
his Introduction to Gierke's *Political Theories of the
Middle Ages* he was disposed to ascribe no small part
of this confusion to the timidity "tardily redressed by
the invention of Parish Councils" which had stood
between the English village and legal personality.

Other defects of loose and imperfect thinking upon
the Corporation were pointed out to the readers of the
Law Quarterly Review in the articles entitled the
"Corporation Sole and the Crown as Corporation."
The American State has private rights; it has power
to sue; English law, on the other hand, had never yet

formally admitted that the Corporate realm, besides being the wielder of public power, might also be the subject
of private rights, the owner of lands and chattels.   Our
habit is to speak of the Sovereign as a corporation sole,
and to refuse to recognise him as the head of a complex
and highly organised "corporation aggregate of many."
Such modes of thought, however well they may have
fitted the designs of Tudor despotism, were neither
appropriate to the needs of a free community nor
adjusted to the conditions of modern life.   The talk
about " Kings who do not die, who are never under
age, who are ubiquitous, who do no wrong and think
no wrong " had "not been innocuous"; and other
practical inconveniences were involved in the identifi-
cation of the Commonwealth with the person of the
Sovereign and in the failure to discriminate between
the natural and official aspects of the Sovereign's personality.   Special legislation, for instance, had been
required to secure private estates for Kings.   For these
insular peculiarities there were, of course, assignable
historical reasons, and one of these reasons, which
Maitland was the first to suggest, is certainly very
curious.   The idea of treating the King of England as
a corporation sole had occurred to Coke, or some other
lawyer of Coke's day, because the parson had already
been treated as a corporation sole.   Why, when and
how the parson came so to be treated furnishes matter
for a very pretty piece of historical investigation.   Who
would have imagined that an unfortunate analogy,
striking across the mind of a Tudor lawyer, would
have helped to give to the legal aspect of the English
State a peculiar colour—a colour different from that

which it has received, for instance, in America. Without a superb knowledge of the Year Books, who could have fixed the offence upon Richard Broke or upon one of Richard Broke's contemporaries? And how many men, having mastered the recondite knowledge of the Year Books, would have retained a sense of the large perspectives of history sufficiently strong and vivid as to apprehend the successive legal and political forces which gave support to a "juristic abortion" through three and a half centuries of national life?

Apart from their interest for the professional student of legal antiquities, Maitland's papers upon Trust and Corporation possess an enduring value by reason of the fine touches of legal and historical perception which are scattered so freely through them. A collection of acute and brilliant observations might without difficulty be made from this as from any other portion of his historical work. "All that we English people mean by religious liberty has been intimately connected with the making of Trusts. Persons who can never be in the wrong are useless in a Court of law. The making of grand theories has never been our strong point. The theory which lies upon the surface is sometimes a borrowed theory which has never penetrated far, while the really vital principles must be sought for in out of the way places. A dogma is of no importance unless and until there is some great desire within it. *Quasi* is one of the few Latin words that English lawyers really love. English history can never be an elementary subject. We are not logical enough to be elementary." Such phrases, even if detached from their context, have a life of their own, but they cannot be so detached without the loss of the greater part of their significance.   An epigram may be an extraneous flourish as irrelevant to all substantial purpose as the ornament of the bad architect.   Maitland's wit was seldom otiose ; it was a shining segment in the solid masonry of argument.

In the summer of 1907 Maitland delivered the Rede Lecture at Cambridge, choosing for his theme English Law and the Renaissance.   It was his object to show how, when Humanism was reviving the study of Roman law, when Roman law was expelling German law from Germany and winning victories over the relics of Anglo-Norman custom in Scotland, England succeeded in preserving her medieval law books despite their bad Latin and their worse French.   The secret was to be found in an institution peculiar to this country, in the existence of the Inns of Court. " Unchartered, unprivileged, unendowed, without remembered founders, these groups of lawyers formed themselves, and in course of time evolved a scheme of legal education ; an academic scheme of the medieval sort, oral and disputatious....We may well doubt whether aught else would have saved English law in the age of the Reception."   But the lecture, though based upon minute enquiries, was not purely historical.   After pointing out that a hundred legislatures were now building on that foundation of English law—"the work which was not submerged"—Maitland surveyed the prospects for the future and pronounced that the unity of English law was precarious.   Queensland had made her own penal code in 1895 ; other colonies might follow in the same way.   The Germans, "by a mighty effort of science and forbearance," had unified their law upon a national and historical basis. Might not the British Parliament endeavour to put out work which would be a model for the British world ? " To make law that is worthy of acceptance for free communities that are not bound to accept it, this would be no mean ambition. *Nihil aptius, nihil efficacius ad plures provincias sub uno imperio retinendas et fovendas.* But it is hardly to Parliament that one's hopes must turn in the first instance." Certain ancient and honourable societies, proud of a past that is unique in the history of the world, may become fully conscious of the heavy weight of responsibility that was assumed when English law schools saved, but isolated, English law in the days of the Reception. " In that case the glory of Bruges, the glory of Bologna, the glory of Harvard, may yet be theirs." The lecturer paused, and then surveying the crowded Senate House added, with an effect which those who heard him cannot forget, certain words which have not been printed. " But," he concluded, " I see, Mr Vice-Chancellor, that strangers are present."

XII.

With health so broken that even the summers in England seldom passed without periods of illness and pain Maitland embarked upon one of the great undertakings of his life, an edition of the *Year Books of Edward II.* " These Year Books are a precious heritage. They come to us from life. Some day they will return to life once more at the touch of some great historian." The spirit in which Maitland approached the work is indicated by two quotations, the first from Roger North, the second from Albert Sorel, which are printed on the title page of each volume. "He (Sergeant Maynard) had such a relish of the old Year Books that he carried one in his coach to divert him in travel, and said he chose it before any comedy." "C'est toute la tragédie, toute la comédie humaine que met en scène sous nos yeux l'histoire de nos lois. Ne craignons pas de le dire et de le montrer." The edition of these Year Books printed in the reign of Charles II. from a single inferior manuscript was imperfect and bad. Maitland determined to show how an edition should be made, and in his eyes no labour was too great for such a task. These records were unique, priceless, imcomparable. "Are they not the earliest reports, systematic reports, continuous reports, of oral debate? What has the whole world to put by their side? In 1500, in 1400, in 1300, English lawyers were systematically reporting what of interest was said in Court. Who else in Europe was trying to do the like, to get down on paper and parchment the shifting argument, the retort, the quip, the expletive? Can we, for example, hear what was really said in the momentous councils of the Church, what was really said in Constance and Basel, as we can hear what was really said at Westminster long years before the beginning of 'the conciliar age'?" The Year Books contained more medieval conversation than had survived in any other authentic source. The history of law could not be written without them. "Some day it will seem a wonderful thing that men once thought that they could write the history of medieval England without the Year Books."

The Reports began in 1285, and from 1293 the stream was fairly continuous. "This surely is a memorable event. When duly considered it appears as one of the great events in English History. To-day men are reporting at Edinburgh and Dublin, at Boston and San Francisco, at Quebec and Sydney and Cape Town, at Calcutta and Madras. Their pedigree is unbroken and indisputable. It goes back to some nameless lawyers at Westminster to whom a happy thought had come. What they desired was not a copy of the chilly record, cut and dried, with its concrete particulars concealing the point of law : the record overladen with the uninteresting names of litigants and oblivious of the interesting names of sages, of justices, of sergeants. What they desired was the debate with the life-blood in it, the twists and turns of advocacy, the quip courteous and the countercheck quarrelsome. They wanted to remember what really fell from Bereford, C. J., his proverbs, his sarcasms : how he emphasised a rule of law by *Noun Dieu* or *Par Seint Piere*! They wanted to remember how a clever move of Sergeant Herle drove Sergeant Toudeby into an awkward corner, or how Sergeant Passeley invented a new variation on an old defence : and should such a man's name die if the name of Ruy López is to live ?"

Maitland lived to complete three volumes of the Year Books. The French was printed on one side of the page, a translation executed in terse and faithful

English on the other.   Those who were familiar with
the work of the Literary Director of the Selden Society
had no cause for surprise at the exquisite finish of the
editing.   They were prepared for an elaborate *apparatus criticus*, for a careful account of the manuscripts,
and for such notes as might be requisite to explain
allusions and to elucidate obscurities.   The great
discovery, that the Reports were not official records
but the private note books of law students, was so
entirely in Maitland's happy and characteristic vein,
that, although no one else had earned the title to
make it, it was quite natural that it should be made
by him.   But there was one feature in the Introduction
to the first volume which startled even his admirers.
The editor took occasion to settle the grammar and
syntax of the Anglo-French language, its nouns and
its verbs, its declensions and its tenses.   His friends
had known him as lawyer, historian, diplomatist,
paleographer, and no exhibition of excellence in any
one of these departments would have afforded them
the slightest sensation of novelty ; but they had not
divined in him the philologist and grammarian.

In answer to surprised congratulations, he said,
with the quick sparkle of humour which his friends
knew so well, that he would go down to posterity as
the author of " Maitland's law "; he had discovered
that such few Anglo-French verbs as possessed "an
imperfect on active service" rarely employed their
preterites.   The experts in medieval French have
applauded the work, and the editors of the *Cambridge
History of English Literature* have thought good to
reprint it.   In the course of a winter spent under a

blue sky Maitland had made a really important contribution to medieval philology. And yet, far as he carried his investigations into the forms, the structure, and the orthography of the language which he found in his manuscripts of the fourteenth century, philology was not the primary object of his quest. He wished to edit his text as well as it was capable of being edited, and to provide guidance for those who should take up the work when he was no longer there to direct it. The French text of the Year Books was full of abbreviations which could not be expanded unless the forms of the language were accurately ascertained. Maitland therefore applied himself to learn whatever might be learned about them. The work was pioneer work, very minute and laborious, but for Maitland a labour of love. The men who wrote this forgotten and unexplored language were often clumsy and careless scribes. Their spelling was full of vagaries; there was no word so short but that they would spell it in several ways; through neglect of the "e" feminine they lost not entirely but very largely their sense of gender; they would murder the infinitive; they coined strange terminations out of misunderstood contractions; but they were using a living tongue to describe law that was alive; and if in some ways a fine language degenerated in the current usage of the English Courts, healthy processes were at work determining the use of words, processes which it was worth while to watch with some narrowness, for if thought fashions language, language in turn reacts upon thought.

"Let it be that the Latin and French were not of a very high order, still we see at Westminster a cluster of men which deserves more attention than it receives from our unsympathetic, because legally uneducated, historians. No, the clergy were not the only learned men in England, the only cultivated men, the only men of ideas. Vigorous intellectual effort was to be found outside the monasteries and universities. These lawyers are worldly men, not men of the sterile caste; they marry and found families, some of which become as noble as any in the land; but they are in their way learned, cultivated men, linguists, logicians, tenacious disputants, true lovers of the nice case and the moot point. They are gregarious, clubable men, grouping themselves in hospices, which become schools of law, multiplying manuscripts, arguing, learning and teaching, the great mediators between life and logic, a reasoning, reasonable element in the English nation."

Meanwhile health was failing and gaps were being made in the circle of his most intimate friends. Henry Sidgwick, the revered master of philosophy, went first, then Lord Acton, finally, in 1904, Leslie Stephen. Some words which Maitland spoke of Henry Sidgwick have already been quoted in this memoir; they are passionate in the intensity of their affection and regard. Acton was a friend of less ancient standing, who by his high character and vast learning had conquered Maitland's unreserved enthusiasm; the loss of Leslie Stephen was mourned as that of a near relative. Of these deaths one was a possible and the other an actual cause of some deviation from Maitland's appointed course of legal work. Upon the vacancy in the Cambridge Chair of Modern History which occurred in 1902, Maitland was invited by Mr Balfour to succeed

Acton. The appointment would have been applauded throughout the historical world, but Maitland felt that his health was too precarious to admit of his undertaking the labours of a new Chair. Besides, there were the Year Books ; there were the illusive and fascinating subtleties of the *persona ficta*. He would not lightly abandon the law. *Nolumus leges Angliæ mutare*, he wrote to a friend, with a slight variation on the classic words of those English barons who in the reign of Henry III. resisted the introduction of a foreign usage. The decision was doubtless wise, but the continuity of Maitland's legal work was not destined to remain unbroken. Leslie Stephen had expressed a wish that, if any appreciation of him were published, it should be done by Maitland. "He, as I always feel, understands me." Such a call could not be neglected, and so the Year Books were laid aside, or rather the pace was slackened, while Maitland laboured with loving and scrupulous diligence upon the *Life and Letters of Leslie Stephen*.

To those who knew Leslie Stephen best the biography has seemed to be a true and vivid picture of the man ; yet the work was undertaken with many misgivings, and gave cause for much anxiety. In the editing of the Year Books Maitland was exercising his own familiar craft, and doing what no other living man could do so well ; but the writing of biography was new ground, and Maitland felt uncertain of his powers. The task was rendered more difficult by the depth of Maitland's affection for Stephen, and by his scrupulous anxiety to write down no epithet or adverb which would have seemed to Stephen himself to be excessive. Then there were the thousand and one little questions of taste and judgment which always confront the biographer. Should such a passage be omitted in deference to so and so's feelings? Will such and such a letter, interesting though it be to an intimate friend, commend itself to the chance reader? A man in the full tide of vigour might have shouldered the labour without a twinge of self-criticism, but Maitland, who was very ill and full of a most delicate and sensitive modesty, felt the burden of responsibility. "He is too big for me for one sort of writing and too dear for another," he wrote to a friend; and only when a considerable portion of the book had received the approval of relatives did he begin to experience a sensible measure of relief. The steady appreciation of Miss Caroline Stephen, and some warm words written by Lady Ritchie, brought him peculiar pleasure. .

The *Life and Letters of Leslie Stephen* appeared in the autumn of 1906, and reviews were steadily flowing in when the Downing household began to make preparations for its annual pilgrimage across the sea. Maitland, who was greatly relieved at the publication of his book, and at its friendly reception in the press, seemed to have recovered something of his old buoyancy. He pushed on an edition of Sir Thomas Smith's *De Republica Anglorum*, which a pupil was undertaking at his instigation and under his supervision, and renewed his attack upon the Year Books. For some years past he had been concerned with the prospect of finding a trained scholar who would be capable of carrying on the work when he was no longer there to direct it. In a foreign university a man of Maitland's power would have created a school; young men from all parts of the country would have clustered round him to learn paleography and law French, and the elements of social and legal history, and the zeal of the class would have atoned for any deficiency in numbers. But the climate of the English University is not favourable to the production of finished historical technique. We are an economical race, and since advanced work does not pay in the Tripos, or in the careers to which the Tripos serves as a portal, it is left to the casual patronage of amateurs. Maitland thoroughly understood the practical limitations under which an English professor must work. He gave courses of lectures which were expressly adapted to the general needs of the undergraduates, and were attended by all the law students in the University, but interspersed these general courses with others of a more special character, designed to interest the real historical student. Thus, in 1892 and 1894, he held classes for the study of English Medieval Charters, and this instruction in paleography and diplomatic was repeated in 1903, 1904 and 1905. In sixty hours spent over facsimiles Maitland contended that he could turn out a man who would be able to read medieval documents with fluency and exactitude.

But with two exceptions the contributors to the volumes of the Selden Society were not drawn from the ranks of Maitland's Cambridge pupils, and the completion of the fourth volume of the Year Books was undertaken by a distinguished scholar, who, though he would be the first to admit that he had learnt much of his craft from Maitland, was never an academical pupil in the strict sense of the term.

One Cambridge disciple there was, who, under Maitland's guidance, attained to rare distinction.

Miss Mary Bateson was writing essays for Maitland while he was Reader in English Law, and at that early period impressed him with the thoroughness and grasp of her knowledge.   Under Maitland's direction Miss Bateson became one of the best medievalists in England.   Her industry rivalled that of her master; her judgments were sane and level, and in the art of historical editing she acquired almost all that Maitland could teach her.   Articles and volumes flowed from her pen, all of them good, but best of all the two volumes upon Borough customs, published by the Selden Society in 1904 and 1906, and owing much "to the counsel and direction of Professor Maitland." Then very suddenly, in the late autumn of 1906, Miss Bateson died.   Maitland was already preparing to sail for the Canaries, whither his wife and elder daughter had preceded him.   The loss of Miss Bateson affected him deeply.   He found time to write two short notices for the Press, speaking of qualities which had impressed him, "the hunger and thirst for knowledge, the keen delight in the chase, the good-humoured willingness to admit that the scent was false, the eager desire to get on with the work, the cheerful resolution to go back and begin again, the broad good sense and the unaffected modesty," and then embarked for Southampton.   Friends who saw him upon the eve of his departure spoke of him hopefully: for judged by his own frail standard he seemed to be well.   Then came a telegram announcing his death.   On the voyage out he had developed or contracted pneumonia, and being alone and ill-cared for, arrived at Las Palmas desperately ill.   His wife flew down from the villa which she had prepared against his coming, but the malady had obtained too firm a hold, and he died on December 19, 1906, at Quiney's Hotel. His body lies in the English cemetery at Las Palmas. At the time of his death he was fifty-six years of age.

He was not without honour in his own generation. In that inclement December five invitations travelled out to Las Palmas,—from the University of Oxford that he should deliver the Romanes lecture, and from the United States of America that he should lecture at the Lowell Institute, at Harvard, and at the Universities of Columbia and Chicago. Academic honours had come to him in plenty. Cambridge and Oxford, Glasgow, Moscow and Cracow gave him their honorary degrees. He was corresponding member of the Royal Prussian and of the Royal Bavarian Academies, distinctions rarely conferred upon English scholars, an honorary Fellow of his old College, Trinity, an honorary Bencher of Lincoln's Inn, an original Fellow of the British Academy. The newly established bronze medal of the Harvard Law School was awarded to him in the last days of his life, and on the news of his death movements were set on foot at each of the great English Universities to do honour to his memory. At a public meeting held in the Hall of Trinity College, Cambridge, on June 1, 1907, and addressed by some of the most eminent representatives of English learning it was resolved that "a Frederic William Maitland Memorial Fund should be established for the promotion of research and instruction in the history of law and legal language and institutions, and that this should be supplemented by a personal memorial to be placed in the Squire Library of the University[1].

[1] A bronze bust, executed by Mr S. Nicholson Babb, has, in

At Oxford some students of law and history contributed to form a library of legal and social history
to be called the Maitland Library, and to be connected
with the Corpus Chair of Jurisprudence now held by
Professor Vinogradoff. By the kindness of the
Warden and Fellows of All Souls a room was lent
to the Maitland Library in the front quadrangle of the
College, and there the student may find Maitland's
own copy of *Domesday Book*, together with many
other volumes which had been in his possession and
which bear the traces of his usage. As a token of his
respect for Maitland's memory, and to further the
skilled editing of a valuable repertory of knowledge,
Mr Seebohm has presented to the Maitland Library
his famous manuscript of the Denbigh Cartulary, one
of the cardinal authorities for the history of Welsh
land-tenures, and an edition of this collection of documents, executed by the pupils of the Corpus professor,
will be the most appropriate tribute to Maitland's
example in a University in which he might have been,
but was not, an adopted son.

Lord Acton once spoke of " our three Cambridge
historians, Maine, Lightfoot, Maitland," each a pioneer
in his own region of research, and each a name of
significance for universal history. Maitland was not
a Conservative like Maine, or a Churchman like
Lightfoot ; he was simply a scientific historian, with
a singularly open and candid mind, and with a de-
tachment almost unique from the prejudice of sect
or party. In politics he would have ranked himself
as a Liberal Unionist, though his mind was far too

pursuance of this resolution, been presented to the University by
the subscribers to the fund and is placed in the Squire Law Library.

independent to bear the strain of party allegiance and
led him to differ upon some important questions from
the principles upheld by the Unionist government.
Thus he was in favour of what is called "the secular
solution" in education, and tried, but without success,
to think well of the policy which brought about the
South African War. The Protectionist reaction excited
his disapproval, and he joined a Free Trade Committee
in Cambridge : but he rarely spoke of politics, and like
all men of the scientific temperament had small interest
in the party game, and no little diffidence as to his
power of reaching solid conclusions upon questions
which he had not the leisure thoroughly to explore. But upon matters which affected the interests
of knowledge and education his views were firm and
clear-cut.

His place in the history of English law has been
summarized by Professor Dicey with an authority to
which I can make no pretence. "Maitland's services
to law were at least threefold. He demonstrated in
the first place what many lawyers must have suspected,
that law could contribute at least as much to history as
history could contribute to law. Now that the truth of
this assertion has been proved it seems a commonplace
to insist upon it. But if one looks at the works of
our best historians, even of so great an historian as
Macaulay, who had rare legal capacity, and who had
extensive knowledge from some points of view of
English law, one is astonished to observe how small
a part law was made to play in the development of the
English nation, which had been, above all, a legal-
minded nation. The doctrine that law was an essential
part of history needed not only asserting—we could all

probably have done this—but demonstrating. The needed demonstration has been made by Maitland, and will not be forgotten. Maitland's second achievement is this : law ought to be, but hitherto in England has not been, a part of the literature of England. Among Maitland's predecessors two men living in different ages have done their best to make law a part of the literature of England. You will forgive me for commemorating, as in my case is almost a matter of private duty, the noble effort made by Blackstone to give law its rightful position in the world of letters. Blackstone failed, not by any weakness of his own, but because he left no successors. He did as much as a man could achieve in Blackstone's time. Maitland himself, I believe, shared this opinion. The next man who took in hand a book somewhat similar to that undertaken by Blackstone was Sir Henry Maine. He achieved a great measure of success. He stimulated in a way which it was difficult for anyone to realise who had not read Maine's *Ancient Law* when it first appeared, public interest in law and jurisprudence. He gave to the English world a new view of the possibilities of interest possessed by the study of law. But his success is not complete. He did not show, as did Maitland, that even the most crabbed details of English law might be made part of English literature. The reason why Maine cannot in this matter stand on the same level with Maitland is that he did not possess the qualifications for the third and last of Maitland's great achievements. No one can say that profound learning was possessed by either Blackstone or Sir Henry Maine. But Maitland was a learned historian as well as a learned lawyer. He therefore could and did demonstrate that extraordinary learning and research have no connection whatever with dullness and pedantry, and that learning may be combined with the most philosophic and the profoundest views of law which the mind of man can form[1]."

This sketch will have been written in vain if it fails to suggest that the world lost in Maitland not only a great and original scholar but also a nature of singular charm and beauty. The life of severe scholarship may, and perhaps often does, dry up the fountains of sympathy, but this was not the case with Maitland. The current of his affections ran deep and strong, and so easily was his enthusiasm fired that he would praise the books of young authors with a delight which seemed almost unqualified if they happened to contain any real merit. No one was more entirely free from self-importance or from any desire to defend, after they had become untenable, positions which he had once been inclined to maintain. He possessed a gift which is far rarer than it is generally supposed to be, and is often very imperfectly possessed by learned men, an intense and disinterested passion for truth, a passion so pure that he would speak with genuine enthusiasm of such criticisms of his own work as he judged to be well founded and to constitute a positive addition to knowledge. His modesty, both in speech and writing, was so extreme that it might have been put down to affectation ; but it was an integral part of the temper which made him great in scholarship. He saw the vast hive of science and the infinite garden of things, and knew how little the most busy life could add to the store ; and so, living always in the company of

[1] *Cambridge University Reporter*, July 22, 1907, p. 1308.

large projects and measuring himself by the highest standard of that which is obtainable in knowledge, he viewed his own acquisitions as a small thing—a fragment of light won from a shoreless ocean of darkness.

His peculiar genius lay in discovery. He thought for himself, wrote a pure nervous English of his own, and even in the ordinary converse of life gave the impression of a being to whom everything was fresh and alive. His style was very characteristic of his vivid and elastic mind, ranging as it did from grave eloquence to colloquial fun, and using only the simplest vocabulary to produce its effects. Conscious theory or method of style he neither claimed nor cared to possess; he wrote as the spirit moved him, finding with astonishing ease the vestment most appropriate to his thought, and composing with such fluency that his manuscript went to press almost free of erasures. The literary and artistic conventions of the hour did not appeal to him. He never went to picture galleries; in later life he seldom read poetry, though as a boy he had been fond of it; and he would profess to be unable to distinguish a good sonnet when he saw one. Knowing the thing which he could do best, and judging that it was worthy of a life, he stripped himself of all superfluous tastes and inclinations that his whole time and strength might be dedicated to the work. Even music had to give way. And yet, though he laboured under the spur of a most exacting conscience and with every discouragement which illness and harrowing physical pain could oppose, it was with a certain blithe alacrity, as if work, however protracted and monotonous, was always a delightful pastime. He would sit in an armchair with a pipe in his mouth and some ponderous folio propped against his knees, steadily reading and smoking far into the night, thinking closely, taking no note, but apparently retaining everything. For a man who wrote and taught so much his knowledge was amazing both in range and accuracy; but his panoply might have been of gossamer so lightly did he bear it, and those who saw him a few times only may remember him chiefly for his irrepressible gift of humour, or for some external features, the fine steady brown eye, the rich flexible voice, the pale clear cut face seamed with innumerable lines, which lit up so quickly in the play of talk. Mr S. H. Butcher, who was in the same year at Cambridge and of the same college, has spoken the mind of those who knew him best. "When they think of him they recall, in the first instance, the delightful companion, the friend who had himself the genius of friendship. They think of his humour, overflowing from his talk and his speeches into what seems to many the driest regions of legal or antiquarian learning, and they recall his modesty, his quiet charm and his essential courtesy of soul[1]." And there was withal that high spiritual power of abnegation and of purpose in which the lover of hard won truth attains to his beatitude. *Res severa est verum gaudium.*

---

[1] *Cambridge University Reporter*, July 22, 1907, p. 1306.

BIBLIOGRAPHICAL NOTE

Among the many appreciations of Maitland's work which have appeared in print the following may be specially noticed: *Quarterly Review*, April, 1907 (Sir F. Pollock); *Proceedings of the British Academy*, 1905–6 (Sir F. Pollock); *English Historical Review*, April, 1907 (P. Vinogradoff); *Selden Society Year Books Series*, vol. IV., Preface (B. F. Lock, with reproduction of a portrait by Miss Beatrice Lock); *Solicitors' Journal*, Jan. 5, 1907 (B. F. L.); *Law Quarterly Review*, April, 1907 (a series of appreciations by foreign jurists); *Political Science Quarterly*, June, 1907 (American impressions); *Cambridge University Reporter*, 22 July, 1907 (Report of the Proceedings at a Meeting for promoting a Memorial of the late Frederic William Maitland); *Juridical Review*, April, 1907 (D. P. Heatley); *Frederic William Maitland*—Two Lectures and a Bibliography by A. L. Smith, Oxford, 1908; *Peerage and Pedigree*, by J. H. Round, vol. I., p. 146, London, 1910.

For EU product safety concerns, contact us at Calle de José Abascal, 56–1°,
28003 Madrid, Spain or eugpsr@cambridge.org.